D1594500

KANT'S FINAL SYNTHESIS

KANT'S FINAL SYNTHESIS

An Essay on the *Opus postumum*

ECKART FÖRSTER

HARVARD UNIVERSITY PRESS
Cambridge, Massachusetts
London, England
2000

Printed in the United States of America

Library of Congress Cataloging-in-Publication Data

Förster, Eckart.
  Kant's final synthesis : an essay on the Opus postumum / Eckart Förster.
    p. cm.
  Includes bibliographical references (p.) and index.
  ISBN 0-674-00166-4 (cloth : alk. paper)
    1. Kant, Immanuel, 1724–1804. Opus postumum. 2. Transcendentalism.
  3. Physics—Philosophy. I. Title.

B2794.O63 F67 2000
193—dc21   99-059804

For Kira

Contents

Preface

Nearly eighty years after Kant's death, a provincial Prussian journal, the *Altpreußische Monatsschrift,* published in a number of installments selections from a manuscript on which Kant had worked for more than the last decade of his life. To his colleagues and former pupils, Kant had often spoken with enthusiasm of this work, describing it as the keystone of his entire system and as the chef d'oeuvre that was to demonstrate conclusively the tenability and real applicability of his philosophy. Yet after his death the whereabouts of the manuscript, which Kant had no longer been able to edit himself, remained unknown for half a century. When it finally resurfaced, the chronological order of the various sheets and fascicles had been completely corrupted. Preparing even parts of the text for publication seemed such an impossible task that one of the initial editors at the *Altpreußische Monatsschrift* refused to have his name attached to the publication and soon resigned in frustration.

The comprehensibility of the text was scarcely improved when in the late 1930s the entire manuscript, in the jumbled order in which it had been transmitted, became available as Kant's *Opus postumum* in the edition of the Royal Prussian Academy of Science. Early readers compared the challenge of making sense of Kant's last work to that of crossing an uncharted desert, or of inferring the pattern of an oriental rug from the confusing array of knots on its back. In view of the extraordinary problems the text imposed on its student, Heinz Heimsoeth, himself one of the foremost Kant scholars of his time, contended that a comprehensive understanding of Kant's last philosophical period could come only from a number of short monographic studies of limited, well-defined problems in this text. His advice was not well taken, however, and Kant's last work remained the terra incognita of Kant scholarship for years to come.

When entrusted with the task of preparing an English edition of a selection of Kant's *Opus postumum*, I decided to follow Heimsoeth's advice. Tackling several of its key topics in a number of short essays seemed the best, if not the only, way to come to a genuine understanding of the problems shaping the last phase of Kant's philosophical career. That required, first and foremost, relating them to Kant's published writings. Very soon it became clear that just as Kant's earlier major publications contain the key to an understanding of his last work, the *Opus postumum* also sheds remarkable new light on these earlier works—works that we believe we know quite well.

Some of those essays form the basis of the present book. They have been completely rewritten and supplemented, in most cases substantially, with new material. The last two chapters are based on articles composed after the edition had been completed. Throughout this book I have aimed to make as explicit and transparent as possible the connections between Kant's *Opus postumum* and his earlier works, and to illuminate the extraordinary continuity and inner dynamics of his transcendental philosophy as it progresses toward its final synthesis.

Since the present study is the first book in English devoted entirely to the *Opus postumum* and its place in the Kantian corpus, I have sought to highlight in particular two of its features that, in my view, make it unique and altogether different from Kant's earlier works. First, because of its unedited format, the *Opus postumum,* unlike any of his published writings, permits us to observe Kant at work over a period of many years, thus granting us a remarkable insight into his working style and into the genesis of one of his major works—in this case a work that still, to a large extent, remains to be explored. Second, although Kant began this manuscript in order to solve a comparatively minor problem within his philosophy, his reflections soon forced him to readdress virtually all the key problems of his critical philosophy: the objective validity of the categories, the dynamical theory of matter, the nature of space and time, the refutation of idealism, the theory of the self and its agency, the question of living organisms, the doctrine of practical postulates and the idea of God, the unity of theoretical and practical reason, and, finally, the idea of transcendental philosophy itself. In the end, Kant was convinced that these problems, some of which had preoccupied him throughout his career, could finally be brought to a coherent and adequate solution and be integrated into a single philosophical conception. One of my aims in this book is to show that this conviction deserves not only our intellectual respect but also our undivided philosophical attention.

In Chapter 1, I seek to discern what motivated Kant, when the successful completion of his critical philosophy in the form of three *Critiques* already lay behind him, to postpone once again the construction of the system of metaphysics (for which the *Critiques* were merely intended to prepare the ground) and to work instead on a book to be called "Transition from the Metaphysical Foundations of Natural Science to Physics." The project of such a Transition, whose initial conception can have occurred no later than 1790, was intended to supplement the *Metaphysical Foundations of Natural Science;* moreover, it was a work that had to be carried out if Kant was to exhaust the field of possible a priori knowledge in philosophy (as he thought he must). A close examination of the early fascicles of the *Opus postumum* makes clear, however, that during its initial phase Kant lacked any satisfactory principle from which such a Transition could derive its own systematic form and structure.

In Chapter 2, I trace the development of his theory of matter between 1786 and 1799, that is, from the *Metaphysical Foundations of Natural Science* to the publication of the third edition of the *Critique of Judgment,* whose only emendation is one surprising alteration of the text. Following Kant's own suggestion in a letter of 1792 that his earlier explanation of the differences in density of matter is circular, I delineate his attempts to remedy this problem in the early parts of the *Opus postumum.* The resulting theory of matter, which essentially involves the assumption of a universally distributed ether or caloric as the basis of all moving forces of matter, makes intelligible, indeed requires, the correction in the 1799 edition of the *Critique of Judgment.*

Chapter 3 takes as its point of departure Kant's notorious claim, made repeatedly in 1798, that there is a "gap" in his critical philosophy causing him no end of agony and that he hopes to close by means of the work at hand. My interpretation, examining in detail the role the *Metaphysical Foundations* was to play within Kant's critical philosophy, confirms Kant's assessment and suggests that this "gap" has repercussions for the *Critique of Pure Reason* itself, more precisely, for the demonstration of the objective validity of the categories and principles of the understanding.

Chapter 4 divides into two main parts. The first part examines the surprising shift in the status of the ether which occurs in the *Opus postumum* in mid-1799: a shift from being regarded as an inevitable hypothesis for the explanation of physical phenomena to being viewed as a categorically given material whose reality Kant now tries to deduce from the conditions of possible experience. In a close examination of the structure of these proofs, I arrive at the conclusion that Kant's ether in these fascicles is best understood as a transcendental ideal in the sense of the *Critique of Pure Reason*. Moreover, it is precisely the features this "elementary material" has in common with a Kantian ideal that provides the Transition with its long-sought principle. First appearances to the contrary, the ether proofs of the *Opus postumum* do not violate any of the critical standards set by Kant's *Critiques*.

In the second part of Chapter 4, Kant's doctrine of self-positing is reconstructed and analyzed in close relation to the classical statements on transcendental and empirical self-consciousness developed in the *Critique of Pure Reason*. On the interpretation offered here, the doctrine of self-positing complements the position of the first *Critique* while at the same time essentially involving the results established by the ether proofs discussed in the first part of this chapter. By interconnecting in the way described, ether theory and self-positing also provide Kant with the elements required to close the "gap" in his critical philosophy that was the subject of Chapter 3.

Chapter 5, on Kant's theory of practical self-positing, traces the development of his ethico-theology from the first *Critique* to the *Opus postumum* and shows why, at the end of his philosophical career, the doctrine of practical postulates, so central to his earlier ethical writings, is given up. In Kant's final position, ethics and religion coincide—a result, I suggest, that stems as much from the dynamics inherent in his ethico-theology as from developments within the *Opus postumum* itself. The combined theories of theoretical and practical self-positing culminate in an account of transcendental philosophy as a doctrine of ideas, or *Ideenlehre*. In this doctrine Kant's philosophy achieves its long-sought systematic unity, and a problem that had beset him since the first *Critique* receives its overdue solution: the problem of the unity of theoretical and practical reason.

The final chapter assumes a greater distance from the text of the *Opus postumum* than the previous chapters do. Here I relate the theory of the self-constitution of reason to the views of one of Kant's contemporaries, Friedrich Hölderlin, and one of ours, Ludwig Wittgenstein. In this way I seek to illustrate the central assumption that underlies Kant's final synthesis, and to bring to light the strength and weakness of the conception of transcendental philosophy that marks the culmination of his lifelong philosophical reflections.

Material from the following previously published essays has been incorporated in this book with kind permission of the respective editors and publishers:

"Is There 'A Gap' in Kant's Critical System?" *Journal of the History of Philosophy* 25:4 (1987), 533–555.

"Kant's *Selbstsetzungslehre*," in Eckart Förster, ed., *Kant's Transcendental Deductions: The Three Critiques and the Opus postumum* (Stanford: Stanford University Press, 1989), pp. 217–238.

"Die Idee des Übergangs: Überlegungen zum Elementarsystem der bewegenden Kräfte," in Forum für Philosophie Bad Homburg, ed., *Übergang: Untersuchungen zum Spätwerk Immanuel Kants* (Frankfurt: Vittorio Klostermann, 1991), pp. 28–48.

"'Was darf ich hoffen?' Zum Problem der Vereinbarkeit von theoretischer und praktischer Vernunft bei Immanuel Kant," *Zeitschrift für philosophische Forschung* 46:2 (1992), 169–186.

"Kant's Third Critique and the *Opus postumum*," *Graduate Faculty Philosophy Journal* 16:2 (1993), 345–358.

"Ich betrachte die Vernunft, als den Anfang des Verstandes," in G. Derossi, M. M. Olivetti, A. Poma, and G. Riconda, eds., *Trascendenza, Trascendentale, Experienza: Studi in onore di Vittorio Mathieu* (Padua: Cedam, 1995), pp. 299–316.

"Die Wandlungen in Kants Gotteslehre," *Zeitschrift für philosophische Forschung* 52:3 (1998), 341–362.

~◯~

In thinking about Kant's *Opus postumum* I have learned and benefited from numerous colleagues and students. In particular I thank Martin Carrier, Michael Friedman, and Dieter Henrich, with whom I have been able to discuss many aspects of Kant's work and whose criticisms and insights have been invaluable to me.

Abbreviations and Translations

References to Kant's works are given in the text, by volume and page number of the Academy edition of *Kants gesammelte Schriften* (Berlin and Leipzig, 1900–). In the case of Kant's *Opus postumum,* for those passages not included in the English translation of the text, the reference to the Academy edition also specifies the line number; for the translated passages, the page number of the translation is given following the abbreviation "Op." References to the *Critique of Pure Reason* are to the paginations of the first (1781) and second (1787) editions, indicated as "A" and "B," respectively.

I have relied heavily on the already existing and sometimes excellent translations of Kant's works into English, but have deviated from them when I felt, rightly or wrongly, that I could improve on what they offered. The translations consulted are given below, with their corresponding Academy volume and page numbers on the left:

1:385–416   *A New Exposition of the First Principles of Metaphysical Knowledge* (Nova dilucidatio), trans. John A. Reuscher, in *Kant's Latin Writings,* ed. Lewis White Beck (New York: Peter Lang, 1986).

1:473–488   *Physical Monadology* (Monadologia physicam), in *Kant's Latin Writings,* trans. and ed. Lewis White Beck (New York: Peter Lang, 1986).

2:63–164   *The One Possible Basis for a Demonstration of the Existence of God,* trans. Gordon Treash (New York: Abaris Books, 1979).

A/B   *Critique of Pure Reason,* trans. Norman Kemp Smith (London: Macmillan, 1929).

4:253–384   *Prolegomena to Any Future Metaphysics,* trans. Paul Carus and Lewis White Beck (Indianapolis: Bobbs-Merrill, 1950).

4:385–464   *Groundwork of the Metaphysic of Morals,* trans. H. J. Paton (London: Hutchinson's, 1948).

4:465–566   *Metaphysical Foundations of Natural Science,* trans. James Ellington (Indianapolis: Hackett, 1970).

5:1–164   *Critique of Practical Reason,* trans. Lewis White Beck (Indianapolis: Bobbs-Merrill, 1956).

5:165–486   *Critique of Judgment,* trans. James Meredith (Oxford: Oxford University Press, 1952); trans. Werner S. Pluhar (Indianapolis: Hackett, 1987).

6:1–202   *Religion within the Boundaries of Mere Reason,* trans. George di Giovanni, in *The Cambridge Edition of the Works of Immanuel Kant* (Cambridge: Cambridge University Press, 1996).

6:203–494   *Metaphysics of Morals,* trans. Mary J. Gregor (Philadelphia: University of Pennsylvania Press, 1964).

7:117–334   *Anthropology from a Pragmatic Point of View,* trans. Mary J. Gregor (The Hague: Nijhoff, 1974).

8:131–148   *What Does It Mean to Orient Oneself in Thinking?* trans. Allen W. Wood, in *The Cambridge Edition of the Works of Immanuel Kant* (Cambridge: Cambridge University Press, 1996).

8:341–386   *To Perpetual Peace,* in *Perpetual Peace and Other Essays,* trans. and ed. Ted Humphrey (Indianapolis: Hackett, 1983).

10–12   *Kant: Philosophical Correspondence, 1759–99*, partly trans. Arnulf Zweig (Chicago: University of Chicago Press, 1967).

20:195–251   *First Introduction to the "Critique of Judgment,"* trans. Werner S. Pluhar, in *Critique of Judgment* (Indianapolis: Hackett, 1987).

20:257–332   *What Real Progress Has Metaphysics Made in Germany since the Time of Leibniz and Wolff*, trans. Ted Humphrey (New York: Abaris Books, 1983).

21, 22   *Opus postumum*, ed. Eckart Förster, trans. Eckart Förster and Michael Rosen, in *The Cambridge Edition of the Works of Immanuel Kant* (Cambridge: Cambridge University Press, 1993).

27:243–471   "Moral Philosophy Collins," in *Lectures on Ethics*, ed. Peter Heath and J. B. Schneewind, trans. Peter Heath, in *The Cambridge Edition of the Works of Immanuel Kant* (Cambridge: Cambridge University Press, 1997).

29:747–940   "Metaphysics Mongrovius," in *Lectures on Metaphysics*, trans. and ed. Karl Ameriks and Steve Naragon, in *The Cambridge Edition of the Works of Immanuel Kant* (Cambridge: Cambridge University Press, 1997)

              Lectures on Ethics, trans. Louis Infield (New York: Harper & Row, 1963).

In Chapter 6, I use the following additional abbreviations and translations:

StA   Friedrich Hölderlin, *Sämtliche Werke* (Stuttgart: Kohlhammer, 1947–).

H   Friedrich Hölderlin, *Hyperion*, trans. Willard R. Trask, in *Hyperion and Selected Poems*, ed. Eric L. Santner (New York: Continuum, 1990).

PI   Ludwig Wittgenstein, *Philosophical Investigations*, trans. G. E. M. Anscombe (Oxford: Blackwell, 1953).

PG Ludwig Wittgenstein, *Philosophical Grammar,* ed. Rush Rhees, trans. Anthony Kenny (Berkeley: University of California Press, 1974).

Z Ludwig Wittgenstein, *Zettel,* ed. G. E. M. Anscome and G. H. von Wright, trans. G. E. M. Anscome (Oxford: Blackwell, 1981).

All additional translations are my own unless otherwise indicated.

KANT'S FINAL SYNTHESIS

CHAPTER ONE

The Idea of a Transition

In order to form a reliable idea of the importance of Kant's last major work, the so-called *Opus postumum,* it is best to start at the beginning: with the question, that is, why, at the end of his long and distinguished career, Kant intended to write a book with the title "Transition from the Metaphysical Foundations of Natural Science to Physics." In the relevant literature we meet with widespread perplexity as to this question. In 1980, Hansgeorg Hoppe, himself the author of a book on Kant's last work, could still write that our understanding of this text is severely hindered by the fact "that we do not really know exactly from what the Transition commences."[1]

In the three most important recent publications on Kant's *Opus postumum*—the books by Burkhard Tuschling (1971), Vittorio Mathieu (1989), and Michael Friedman (1992)—this question not surprisingly receives quite contrary and incompatible answers. According to Tuschling, the plan for a "science of transition" sprang from Kant's realization that his *Metaphysical Foundations of Natural Science* of 1786 "suffer from incurable internal contradictions."[2] Most prominent among them was the circularity in Kant's account of the attractive force of which he became aware early in the 1790s.[3] This necessitated a revision in his theory of matter that Kant subsequently tried to legitimize by a Transition project conceived entirely for this purpose: "The Transition is . . . designed to justify the necessity of the new undertaking." This means for Tuschling "that the idea of the Transition presupposes the revised theory of matter of the [*Opus postumum*] and can only be understood in terms of it—and cannot, conversely, explain the Transition."[4]

An altogether different suggestion can be found in Mathieu, according to whom the need for a Transition results from Kant's insight into a failure of the *Critique of Judgment*. Since the principles of the *Metaphysical Foundations* had laid the ground only for a science of nature in general, but not for physics as a system of the special laws of nature, Kant tried in the *Critique of Judgment* of 1790 to explain the "unity of the manifold" through a subjective principle of reflective judgment. But soon, Mathieu writes, "Kant regarded the principle of the 'as if' that he had proposed there as no longer satisfactory . . . This thought now appears unsatisfactory to Kant because judgment, if such a principle is assumed, gives a law 'only to itself but not to nature' . . . The unity of the natural world cannot depend on a mere 'as if' ('as if the understanding contained the ground of unity')."[5] And he adds: "This situation, which makes a science of 'Transition' indispensable, is emphasized by Kant after 1796 over and over again."[6]

Michael Friedman, by contrast, sees the origin of Kant's Transition project not in any problem internal to the critical philosophy itself, but in the progress that the natural sciences, in particular chemistry, had made since the publication of the *Metaphysical Foundations*. The new developments initiated by the "chemical revolution" could not be comprehended within the framework of the Newtonian natural philosophy, and since Kant in 1786 had provided a priori foundations only for the

latter, it simply did not "go far enough." It needed to be supplemented with a work that sought "to establish something a
priori" not just with regard to the universal properties of matter in general, but for "the rest of the moving forces that may be
found in nature." Consequently, the Transition project derives,
Friedman writes, "from one of the most important founda-
tional problems facing eighteenth-century science . . . [H]ow
was this brilliantly successful Newtonian paradigm to be extended beyond astronomy and terrestrial mechanics? How, in
particular, were the laws of other types of attractions, such as
those responsible for cohesion or chemical affinities, possibly
to be discovered?"[7]

I can agree with none of these suggestions regarding the
origin of Kant's conception of a Transition. To begin with, on
June 8, 1795, Johann Gottfried Carl Christian Kiesewetter
wrote to Kant: "For some years now you have promised to
present the public with a few sheets that are to contain the
transition from your *Metaphysical Foundation of Natural
Science* to physics itself, which I await eagerly" (12:23). As is
well known, Kiesewetter had studied with Kant in 1788–89
and had visited him again for a month the following fall. Less
well known is the fact that Kant broke off all relations with
Kiesewetter shortly after the visit in 1790, without having
written to him in the meantime.[8] Kant renewed their correspondence in December 1793. Yet there is no mention of a
Transition in this letter, and a later correspondence that might
have been lost would not fit Kiesewetter's expression "for
some years." The tone and wording of Kiesewetter's letter
also rule out the possibility that he might have heard of
Kant's plan through a third person. Thus we must conclude
that Kant had formed the plan for a Transition by at least the
fall of 1790, if not already in the previous year.

This rules out Tuschling's reconstruction of the origin of
the Transition,[9] but Mathieu's suggestion is not thereby immediately eliminated. (I will return to Friedman shortly.) It is

indeed possible that in October 1790 (Kiesewetter's last visit) Kant had already despaired of his third *Critique,* even though it had just been published at Easter of the same year. This is possible, although perhaps not very likely. There is, however, another reason why I think Mathieu's reconstruction is implausible. Mathieu is right, no doubt, in stressing that Kant thought that the systematicity of physics can only be founded a priori, and that its possibility hence had to be explained philosophically. In this vein, the Preface to the second edition of the *Critique of Pure Reason* had already pointed out that physics owes its admirable progress entirely to the insight "that while reason must seek in nature, not fictitiously ascribe to it, whatever as not being knowable through reason's own resources has to be learnt, if learnt at all, only from nature, it must adopt as its guide, in so seeking, that which it has itself put into nature" (Bxiii f.). What it is, however, that reason must put into nature so that physics is not merely an aggregate of perceptions but qualifies as a systematic science of nature, Kant had not said there. The fundamental a priori determinations of a "nature in general" were the proper subject of this book, not the systematic unity of an empirical science.

The *Metaphysical Foundations of Natural Science,* published a year earlier, had provided no real help with this question, either. In its Preface, Kant had indeed emphasized that any genuine science must exhibit both apodictic certainty of its fundamental laws and systematic unity of its cognitions. Moreover, in this work he showed what is to be understood by apodictic certainty in the case of physics. But with regard to the systematic unity of physics, the *Metaphysical Foundations* had little to offer. Its chief concern was the "fundamental determination of a something that is to be an object of the external senses," that is, the determination of the concept of "matter in general" (4:472–479) which Kant carried through according to the four functions of the categories. How beyond this the systematic form of an empirical science might be anticipated a priori he did not know at the time. Even here, however, in the General Observation on Dynamics, Kant did not resist the temptation at least "to present" the moments to which the specific variety of matter must admit of being reduced a priori—and, he added, "as I hope, completely" (4:525). Yet as this hopeful qualification makes clear, he lacked any a priori *principle* of the division and completeness of such moments, any a priori sketch according to which specific varieties of matter might be investigated. At this time, consequently, such "presentation" could amount to little more than what elsewhere he liked to call "a merely random groping among concepts" (Bxv; cf. 4:478, 20:210).

This situation was bound to change with the discovery of reflective judgment as an autonomous faculty.[10] Suddenly it became a priori justified to view nature as purposive and systematic (according to the principle of reflective judgment), whereas from the point of view of determinate judgment it had to be regarded as contingent. That Kant should have felt like putting the new discovery to a concrete use would hardly be surprising. The sudden possibility of progressing beyond where the *Metaphysical Foundations* had to leave off, and of further extending the a priori investigation in the field of corporeal nature, must have stared him in the face. Also, it should be remembered that Kant mentioned the idea of the Transition to Kiesewetter. It was Kiesewetter who—at Kant's own instigation—had read the proofs of the *Critique of Judgment* in Berlin, where it was printed in a great hurry. It seems hardly far-fetched to assume that Kant, when visited by Kiesewetter five months later, should have made this work and its principle of a formal purposiveness of nature the topic of some of their many discussions. From this angle as well it thus seems most likely that it was in the context of their frequent discussions that Kant gave the promise about which Kiesewetter reminded him five years later, namely, to present the public "with a few sheets that are to contain the transition from your *Metaphysical Foundation of Natural Science* to physics itself."

The solution to the problem of the systematicity of physics could thus be assigned to a "science of transition": "The transition from the metaphysical foundations of natural science to physics is the method of bringing about a systematic cognition of physics (which cannot be done through merely collected experiences because the sketch of a system [*der Vorriß eines Systems*] is missing that must be given a priori)" (21: 492.21–24).

"The sketch of a system that must be given a priori": if this is the correct explanation of the origin of Kant's plan for a Transition, it must appear very unlikely indeed that Kant should have thought that the *Critique of Judgment* contained a solution to its problem—a solution with which he subsequently became dissatisfied in Mathieu's sense. For the principle of a formal purposiveness of nature that the power of judgment formulates expresses merely the *precondition* under which the systematicity of an empirical science becomes a priori graspable. Thus Kant wrote in the First Introduction to the *Critique of Judgment:* "it is clear that the nature of reflective judgment is such that it cannot undertake to *classify* the whole of nature by its empirical differentiation unless it assumes that nature itself *specifies* its transcendental laws by some principle . . . The proper [*eigenthümlich*] principle of judgment is thus: Nature, for the sake of judgment, specifies its universal laws to empirical ones, according to the form of a logical system" (20:215f.). This principle allows us for the first time to regard as purposive the part of nature that from the standpoints of the first *Critique* and the *Metaphysical Foundations* had to be regarded as contingent and deterministic. By itself, however, this principle gives no indication as to *how* the physicist must interrogate nature and *what* he has to "put into nature" in order to be systematically instructed

[6]

by her. It "provides no basis for any theory, and it does not contain cognition of any objects and their character any more than logic does" (20:204).[11] Could Kant have been so mistaken? This does not seem very likely, and we should not assume so, I contend, so long as other possible interpretations are open to us.

It may seem now that Friedman's explanation of the origin of Kant's Transition project as an extension of the *Metaphysical Foundations* to the specific variety of nature's forces must be the right one. There is, however, an element in the above reconstruction that he would dispute, namely, the claim that the principle of a formal purposiveness of nature is a new principle that was not available to Kant in 1781, when he wrote the first *Critique*. According to Friedman, the principle of reflective judgment that the third *Critique* establishes is nothing other than a condensed version of reason's principles of homogeneity, variety, and affinity discussed under the heading "The Regulative Employment of the Ideas of Pure Reason" in the Appendix to the Transcendental Dialectic of the *Critique of Pure Reason*: "In other words, what the principle of reflective judgement actually generates here are merely the heuristic or methodological principles presented in the first *Critique* as products of the regulative use of reason at A652–663/B680–691 . . . [I]t in no ways [!] goes beyond the methodological regulative maxims already enumerated in the first *Critique*."[12] Consequently, the relevant conceptual devices were already available to Kant in 1781; reference to his alleged "discovery" of the principle of a formal purposiveness of nature cannot explain the origin of his last work: "It follows, therefore, that the regulative maxims of reflective judgment cannot, by themselves, constitute the key to the Transition project."[13] Its origin must be explained externally and in response to the "developments taking place in the empirical or experimental sciences themselves."[14]

[7]

To assess these claims, it is clear that we must look more closely at the principle of reflective judgment, and at its relation to the regulative ideas of reason.

Let me begin by noting, first, that Kant stated explicitly, and stated repeatedly, that he had "discovered" a *new* a priori principle. When writing to K. L. Reinhold in December 1787, for example, Kant enthusiastically reported the discovery of the new kind of a priori principle which hitherto he had thought "impossible to find." To explore and marvel at what is systematic in knowledge, he predicted, will now give "me ample material for the rest of my life" (10:514).

Second, we must note that it is not reason's own systematic tendencies, nor any teleological reflections, but *natural beauty* that discloses this principle: "Independent natural beauty reveals [*entdeckt*] to us a technic of nature that allows us to represent nature as a system in terms of laws whose principle we do not find anywhere in our understanding" (5:146). What Friedman appears to overlook is Kant's repeated insistence that the principle of a formal purposiveness of nature is disclosed *solely* by aesthetic judgments concerning *natural* beauty. And this discovery was not available at the time of the Appendix to the first *Critique,* because in 1781 Kant still regarded all judgments of taste as "merely empirical" and as barring any a priori sources, as he put it in the footnote to A21. In 1787, for the second edition of the *Critique of Pure Reason,* he revised this footnote (but not the Appendix), acknowledging for the first time that taste has an a priori principle. What kind of principle is this?

A judgment of taste is not a cognitive judgment that determines an object but a judgment in which a subject reports the delight it feels in view of a certain object. Yet such a judgment is not psychological. It differs from all subjective judgments concerning what is agreeable in that it also demands universal agreement: we expect, in expressing a judgment of taste, that anyone aware of the object will agree with us—an expectation we could not reasonably associate with an expression of agreeableness. And it is precisely this universality of the aesthetic judgment that in 1787 Kant realized is a priori in origin and hence demands the "effort of the transcendental philosopher" (5:213; cf. 266) to explain it.

Kant's explanation, briefly, is this. In the cognition of any object, imagination and understanding cooperate, the former combining the manifold that judgment then subsumes under the concept supplied by the latter. If the object is also beautiful, however, judgment realizes that this subsumption does not exhaust the object; rather, it finds in its reflection that understanding and imagination now stand in a "free play" in which the imagination's ability to exhibit representations and the understanding's ability to conceptualize vivify and further each other, mutually stimulating each other to a series of representations and interpretations that are bound by no particular concept (see 5:316). Beauty not only permits but also encourages an imaginative interpretive activity of our faculties that exceeds any conceptual determination. "Taste, as a subjective power of judgment, contains a principle of subsumption, not of intuitions under concepts, but of the *faculty* of intuitions and representation, under the *faculty* of concepts, i.e. the understanding, so far as the former *in its freedom* accords with the latter *in its conformity to law*" (5:287).

Since the judgment of taste is not founded on any concept, it can only be the form of the object on which the free play of imagination and understanding is based. And we consequently expect, even demand,[15] universal agreement in judgments of taste, for these cognitive faculties are assumed to be the same in all human beings. "The quickening of both faculties (imagination and understanding) to an indefinite, but yet, thanks to the given representation, harmonious activity, such as belongs to cognition in general, is the *sensation* whose universal communicability is postulated by the judgment of taste" (5:219).

Moreover, and most important, only beings endowed with imagination and understanding can experience the free play of these faculties, and hence can enjoy the beautiful displays of nature: "Agreeableness holds for nonrational animals too; beauty only for human beings, i.e. beings who are animal and yet rational, though it is not enough that they be rational (e.g., spirits) but they must be animal as well" (5:210). It is as if natural beauty was there for us alone to enjoy, as if nature's forms were designed with a view of *our* faculties. And it is precisely this fact that underlies Kant's "discovery" that natural beauty "reveals" to us a formal purposiveness of nature with regard to *our* power of judgment.

We thus begin to see what Kant means by the formal purposiveness of nature, and how different it is in fact from the logical principles of reason discussed in the Appendix to the Dialectic of the first *Critique.* Natural beauty exhibits a purposiveness in its form that, because entirely contingent from the viewpoint of a transcendental concept of nature, makes the object appear as it were preadapted to our power of judgment, so that this beauty constitutes in itself an object of delight (see 5:245). Because of the actual *experience* of natural beauty, and only because of it, judgment is compelled in its reflection upon nature to adopt as its own principle the view that nature specifies its empirical laws for the purpose of judgment: "So it is actually *only in taste,* more precisely, *only in taste concerning objects of nature,* that judgment reveals itself as a faculty that has its own principle and hence is justified in claiming a place in the general critique of the higher cognitive faculties—a place one might otherwise not have expected for it" (20:244; my italics). This is why Kant can say that the experience of natural beauty "expands" our concept of nature (5:246), although not our knowledge of the objects of nature. It expands the concept of nature from that of a blind mechanism—the concept of nature of the first *Critique* and the *Metaphysical Foundations*—to nature as art, hence to a nature that is *in itself* systematic.

Given this interpretation, one can easily see, contra Friedman, why after 1787 Kant came to realize that a step beyond the *Metaphysical Foundations* can and must be taken. Judgment provides us with a "universal but yet indeterminate principle of a purposive ordering of nature in a system" (20:214). Hence there is still a task to be carried out by the philosopher of the "system from a priori principles" (21: 626.9)—a task, contra Tuschling and Mathieu, which is not as such necessitated by the failure of one of Kant's earlier writings but that marks a genuine desideratum in Kant's system: there must be something like an a priori "elementary system" of the moving forces of matter if physics is to be possible as a systematic science. And we must assume that physics can be systematic, once we have an a priori justification to think that nature itself is systematic, for "there already lies in the concept of the a priori unity of experience . . . the concept of a system of agitating forces of matter as necessarily belonging to experience" (21:596.1–4). Finally, it should not surprise us that Kant initially hoped to carry out this task on "a few sheets": since such an elementary system is to provide the a priori "sketch [*Vorriß*] of a system" but must not transgress into physics itself, it can scarcely become a very sizable project.

And yet, the concept of an "elementary system" is not mentioned in the *Opus postumum* for quite a long time. It is indeed remarkable that Kant's work on the Transition does not commence (as far as we know) until 1796—except for some (albeit important) notes on various loose leaves. Why this lag? A number of different reasons may have contributed to this belated start; I want to mention a perhaps crucial problem whose effect can be witnessed in the *Opus postumum* even after 1796.

"No one attempts to establish a science unless he has an idea upon which to base it," Kant had written in the first *Critique* (A834). Upon what idea, then, is the "science of transition" to be based? The idea—the plan, the principle—according to which such science is to be carried out cannot be derived from the *Metaphysical Foundations of Natural Science,* since the Transition to physics must deal with specifically determined moving forces that can occur *in experience.* The universal concepts of attraction and repulsion of the *Metaphysical Foundations,* however, "furnish no specifically determined, empirical properties," as Kant would write later, "and one can imagine no specific [forces], of which one could know whether they exist in nature, or whether their existence be demonstrable" (22:282, Op. 100).

But likewise, the 'idea' of the Transition cannot be derived from physics, since the Transition itself is to provide the plan for the empirical science of nature.[16] The problem Kant faced thus bore a striking resemblance to the one he had struggled with years before, when he had decided to investigate the very possibility of metaphysics. There, too, he knew that if the enterprise was not to be a colossal *petitio principii* from the start, the inquiry could not itself be metaphysical, nor could the 'idea' according to which it was to be carried out be derived from one of the traditional systems of metaphysics.[17] Just as it took years until Kant saw clearly the "Idea of Transcendental Philosophy" (A1) that "could serve for the Critique of Pure Reason" (A11), it took years (as I will try to show) until Kant was in possession of the 'idea' or the 'principle' that could serve for the transition from the metaphysical foundations of natural science to physics. In the course of these years, what he initially had hoped to present to the public "on a few sheets" grew under his hands into a voluminous manuscript.

The methodological problem Kant took upon himself is indeed considerable. How is one to conduct an a priori science of transition? Where does one commence? And with what? Not surprisingly, Kant felt "that I could not better reach the completeness of a system in the composition of this work, than if here, too, I were to follow the clue given by the categories" (21:311, Op. 25). But even if we assume with Kant that the Transition must proceed from the concept of moving forces of matter, what is to come next? What determinations of moving force in general can we establish when we analyze this concept in accordance with the table of categories? The answer to these questions is indeed anything but clear—so let us turn right away to the first folio draft (mid-1797) of the *Opus postumum* whose very format and outer appearance, with an "Introduction" and continuous numbering of sections, convey an impression of optimism (21:307, Op. 23).[18]

In the first chapter, on "Quantity" (draft "A"), we learn that, since not all matter is homogeneous, its quantity can be determined only through weighing. In the second chapter (draft "B"), Kant defines that with regard to quality, all matter is either solid or fluid, and explains that the droplet-forming property of a fluid is incomprehensible save on the assumption of the living force of a universally distributed caloric *(Wärmestoff)*.[19] This explanation has the additional advantage, Kant points out, "of postulating hypothetically the existence of a particular material required for fluids and thus to indicate [the possibility] of an explanation of a number of appearances from a single principle" (21:319.9–12). He then adds that the rigidification of previously fluid (that is, dissolved in caloric) matter can likewise be explained only through caloric, namely, through its "escape" (21:321.7).

Here the numbering of sections already begins to stagnate, however. On the one hand, caloric is supposed to keep matter fluid and to cause rigidification if it escapes; on the other hand, it cannot itself be fluid since in that case it would itself require a material that made it fluid: "In a word, one cannot form a concept of a caloric, either as an expansive or as an attractive fluid" (21:319.24–320.1). The subsequent §8, "Of the Rigidification *(rigescentia)* of a Fluid Matter," is attempted twice, yet without any noticeable progress. Thus Kant turns to the third chapter, and hence to the category of "Relation" (draft "C"). Under this heading we find him dealing with cohesion, with friction, and—surprisingly—again with rigidity. Does rigidity belong under the second or the third group of categories? With this, draft "C" ends. Kant is silent about "Modality": a draft "D" does not exist.

The next draft ("α") starts all over again. The first chapter, on "Quantity," once again declares that "weighing is the only general and dynamical means for the precise determination of the quantity of matter, of whatever type it be" (22:208, Op. 29). In the second chapter the distinction fluid/solid is once again introduced as the "first division of matter in regard to its quality" (22:213, Op. 32). Yet right away we face the very same problem: "If one assumes an *originally* elastic matter, it would have to be so without caloric . . . The ether would, thus, be the only *originally* elastic matter; the name of fluid would not, however, apply to it" (22:214, Op. 33). Interestingly, this time Kant does not even progress beyond the second category; the subsequent drafts ("β"–"ε") also deal with the problems of fluidity and of solidification.

What these first drafts clearly illustrate, it seems to me, is the total absence of any well-defined idea or principle for the systematic function of the Transition. Most important, the table of categories, constantly invoked by Kant, cannot substitute for the lacking principle and cannot indicate *which* forces must be assembled a priori in the science of transition.

Kant's next draft ("a"–"c") conveys the same impression: under "Quantity" and "Quality" we encounter what is already familiar, including the stagnation in the discussion concerning quality: "Second Attempt: How Is Rigidity of Matter Possible?" (21:276.2–4). The misery is also reflected externally: once again the draft has only *three* parts ("a," "b," "c").[20]

The following draft (which Erich Adickes dates fall 1798) has only three parts ("No. 1," "No. 2," "No. 3"), yet Kant supplements the third part with eight additional drafts ("No. 3α"–"No. 3η," with "β" occurring twice) in which first indications of a turn of events are detectable. Kant begins with renewed reflections on the "quality" and "relation" of matter; for "modality" he records only the heading and outlines a new "Chapter on Quantity" with numbered sections. Surprisingly, the distinction fluid/solid is here subsumed under quantity. What is more interesting, however, is the fact that the ponderability of matter that Kant had previously discussed under this category is now considered in relation to the instrument of weighing. To determine the quantity of matter, Kant writes, we have to presuppose more than gravitational attraction which makes matter heavy. The scale and lever must also be rigid and exercise repulsive force that opposes the weight of the body, "for if the scale or another rigid resistance [*fester Widerstand*] like the lever did not immediately oppose the falling weight by blocking space in this direction, the pressing body would fall right through it. Only because this body is coercible does weighing and the estimation of the quantity of matter become possible" (22:260.2–7).

To this passage Kant adds: "This is mentioned here only so that one can see that the miraculous material of heat exerts its influence not only through the expansion of bodies but also with regard to the estimation of the quantity of matter, by increasing their density" (22:260.10–13). But already on the next sheet (which has the same designation, "No. 3β," and hence either replaces or supplements the previous sheet) we read that the real issue is "how we must think a priori [of moving force] in order to give meaning to the concept of a quantity of matter...which question, since this quantity can only be estimated though *weighing*, is a task for the propaedeutic physiology leading to physics" (22:217.7–11). This thought is quickly extended to the other mechanical powers: all machines, indeed, the whole of mechanics, presuppose *specific* dynamical forces: "N.B. A machine requires (1) rigid (2) cohesive (3) cohesive yet flexible types of matter. (a) the lever (b) rope and block (c) wedge. Pressure, tension, push" (22:259.6–9).

Why this marks a turning point becomes clear if we attend to the precise formulation in which Kant now records the general problem of the Transition: the Transition "must not consist entirely of a priori concepts of matter in general, for in that case it would merely be metaphysics (e.g., if mention is made only of attraction and repulsion in general); nor must it consist entirely of empirical representations, for they would belong to physics...Rather, it must [instruct us with regard] to the a priori principles of the possibility of experience, hence of the investigation of nature" (21:362.28–363.5). Previously, Kant had attempted in vain to arrive at such *Zwischenbegriffe,* or intermediary concepts, of the Transition. One such concept now seems to emerge for the first time, and Kant immediately develops its implications in a number of different formulations—primarily through a critique of the Göttingen mathematician Abraham Kästner. In Volume 2 of Gehler's *Physicalisches Wörterbuch,* a scientific encyclopedia Kant used throughout his work on the Transition, Kästner had been credited with giving the first fully convincing proof for the law of the lever, that is, of the law of equilibrium of forces on the lever on which the whole of statics is built.[21] Kant endorses Gehler's view but points out that Kästner in his proof simply presupposed the rigidity of the lever and ignored the dynamical forces of cohesion required for its stability. Thus Kästner overlooked that without such forces, "no ponderability can be thought, and that one cannot

abstract from this force without losing the concept of ponderability and without contradicting oneself" (21:294.24–26).
To this thought Kant adds in the margin: "The proposition
that all matter is ponderable is not an empirical proposition"
(21:295.22). But neither is it an analytical proposition that
states a necessary inner characteristic of all matter (see 22:
137.17–20). Rather, it expresses the condition under which
experience of the quantity of matter is alone possible. Consequently, the forces that are inseparable from ponderability
cannot be viewed as exclusively empirical, either. For the first
time (if only temporarily), Kant attributes a non-hypothetical
status to caloric which is supposed to make possible the
rigidity of the balance: "It cannot be regarded as a merely hypothetical material" (21:297.10).

Finally, it seems, Kant has found a concept that can be attributed only to the provenience of the Transition—an elementary concept of moving forces that belong "on the one
hand to metaphysics and concepts a priori. On the other
hand to physics as a system from principles of experience,
e.g., the stiffness of the lever" (21:299.10–12). On the next
sheet Kant records: "Thus ponderability (*ponderabilitas*) is
the first function of the moving forces according to the category of quantity. It belongs to both, metaphysics of nature
and physics, and *for this reason* to the transition from the first
to the second" (21:307.4–7; my italics).

Since the division of such forces—forces that are demonstrable only empirically—is to be a priori as well as systematic, it can only take the form of disjunctions: as Kant states
repeatedly, the forces themselves remain *problematic* at this
level (see, for example, 22:357, Op. 116). Consequently, the
"first function" of the Transition is listed as a disjunction: *all
matter is ponderable or imponderable.* The all-penetrating
caloric, whose internal movements are said to make possible
the rigidity of the balance, cannot itself be thought of as ponderable. It penetrates all instruments of measurement. For the

same reason, it cannot be coercible *(sperrbar)*, which must be the case with all ponderable materials. Thus, *all matter is also either coercible or incoercible.* With this, the first elementary concepts of the Transition are secured, and it is telling that Kant now, in these additions to draft "No. 3," also introduces a new concept for the system of the investigation of nature: "Of the *Elementary System* of the Moving Forces of Matter" (21:533.22–23).

This concept did not occur in the earlier drafts, and we may safely assume that it is the external sign of Kant's renewed hope that he might finally solve the problem of the Transition. He begins a new sheet and labels it "1"; on it Kant sketches new Introductions to the entire Transition. Then follow the new drafts with the designations "Elementary System (1–7)." The headings and section numbering indicate the regained élan (see Op. 45–50). Yet with §9 ("Relation"), Kant's work stagnates again. He begins once more with §5: "Third Section: Of the Relation of the Moving Forces of Matter." In the fourth section he only records a definition of modality, then he begins all over again: "Of the Elementary System of the Moving Forces of Matter. First Section: Of the Quantity of Matter in General" (22:150–156). Then Kant crosses out the very first paragraph and begins yet again; shortly after he breaks off altogether. The overall character of the manuscript also changes. Adickes believed he could detect the signs of a "depression" in Kant's changed, now more irregular and even "unattractive" *(unschön)* handwriting.[22]

The reason seems to be clear: Kant had found the first elementary concepts of the Transition, yet in no way were they gained from a principle that would also permit him to derive the remaining concepts. How he should proceed from here— that is, how he might, for instance, derive phenomena of cohesion as relational determinations of matter—was as obscure as ever: the 'idea' of the Transition was still missing. It can hardly surprise us, therefore, if Kant's optimism faded

again and his situation at times looked hopeless and depress-
ing. This situation does not change significantly until mid-
1799 and the drafts "Übergang 1–14" with their ether proofs.
These passages thus occupy a central position in the *Opus
postumum;* Mathieu has rightly and repeatedly insisted on
this point. According to Adickes, on these sheets Kant's
handwriting returns to normal; the lingering "depression"
seems to be over. Since I shall discuss "Übergang 1–14" at
length in Chapter 4, let us for now return to the drafts at
hand. What happens next? Although the pages that follow do
not bring the sought-after principle of the Transition either,
they contain a number of important thoughts of which I
want to mention two.

First, in the new sketches of introductions in which Kant
now tries—once again—to arrive at a general orientation
about his project, we encounter several passages where he appears to reduce the *Metaphysical Foundations of Natural Science* of 1786 to a mere doctrine of motion—passages that
Burkhard Tuschling has made the basis of his interpretation
of the early *Opus postumum.* Although I do not entirely
agree with the interpretation Tuschling offered under the title
Phoronomiekritik, he deserves full credit for having taken se-
riously for the first time Kant's peculiar and ambiguous
descriptions of the *Metaphysical Foundations* in the *Opus
postumum,* rather than following the previously standard
practice of glossing over them with high-handed arrogance as
memory lapses of the "old" Kant. I myself favor a reading of
these Introduction passages that differs from Tuschling's interpretations in the following way.[23]

In these introductions to the Elementary System, the formulation Kant uses to contrast the Transition with the *Metaphysical Foundations* seems important. Whereas the writing
of 1786 allegedly treats only of the concept of matter as the
movable in space, the Transition is said to consider the "extended concept of matter as the movable in space insofar as it

has *moving force*" (22:164.18; see also 163.28; 166.27; 189f., Op. 51, and so on). Yet this is also the First Explication of Mechanics in the *Metaphysical Foundations of Natural Science:* "Matter is the movable insofar as it as such has moving force" (4:536). In the Observation on the Explication Kant wrote: "Now this is the third definition of matter. The merely dynamical concept could also regard matter as at rest . . . [I]n mechanics the force of a matter set in motion is regarded as present in order to impact this motion to another matter. But it is clear that the movable would have no moving force *through its motion* if it did not possess original moving forces."

Can it be surprising if Kant is reminded of this Explication in the course of his reflections on simple machines? For mechanical force or motion is dependent on the *form* of the machine, and this in turn presupposes cohesion of the parts of a matter. Yet in the *Metaphysical Foundations,* Mechanics is based on Dynamics without the possibility of cohesion having been explained there. Even more so: in the Dynamics chapter Kant states that cohesion "does not belong to our present considerations" since it "does not belong to the possibility of matter in general" (4:518). Although this is correct, it does belong to the possibility of matter with a determinate *form*—of a body—and hence to something that can exert moving force through its motion. In this sense Kant now writes: "The movable in space is called 'matter'. Matter, in so far as it has moving force, is, regarded as a whole, a (physical) body" (21:510.26–29). That cohesion "would hence not be metaphysical but physical" (4:518) is thus unjustifiable from the standpoint of the Transition: moreover, the step from Dynamics to Mechanics must now appear as "a leap" that cannot be permitted methodically. It is for this reason, presumably, that in the introduction sketches of the Elementary System, Kant reflects anew on what it means that the movable "as such has moving force"—whereby he finds the answer given in the *Metaphysical Foundations* insufficient in the present context.

Second, there is another important result that begins to emerge in these supposedly stagnating, "depressed" reflections. Each physical body is to be regarded as a system of mechanically moving forces, Kant writes almost in passing, that is, as a machine (22:193, Op. 53n.). This thought is pursued further in succeeding pages, and when its consequences are clear to Kant, he begins an entirely new Elementary System: "A Elem. Syst." On its first sheet, under the heading "According to the Completeness of the Division of the System of Forces in General," Kant notes: "The *final causes* belong equally to the moving forces of nature, whose a priori concept must precede physics, as a clue for the investigation of nature" (21:184, Op. 60). And in the margin he adds:

> Organism is the form of a body regarded as a machine—i.e. as an instrument *(instrumentum)* of motion for a certain purpose ... Mechanism [*Maschinenwesen*] signifies a particular form of the moving forces (set into a certain matter, by nature) which makes them capable of an artificial [motion]—e.g. the stiffness of a lever ... Organic bodies are natural machines, and, like other moving forces of matter, must be assessed according to their mechanical relationships, in the tendency of the metaphysical foundations of natural science [to physics]. (21:185–186, Op. 61)

Compared with the earlier drafts of the *Opus postumum,* these passages indicate a significant change in Kant's position. Previously, organic forces had been excluded from the Transition and assigned to physics. This can no longer be justified once the structural similarity between natural and artificial machines has been noticed: in both cases what concerns us is the derivation of motion "from the specific form of the matter in virtue of which it has particular moving force" (21:187.9–11). In contrast with artificial machines, however, organisms can act as *self-moving* machines (21:194.12).

What seems important to me in this context is that it is Kant's reflections on the ponderability of matter, and on the various mechanical powers, that leads to the inclusion of organic forces into the Elementary System of the Transition. His text, especially in "A Elem. Syst. 1–6," speaks for itself: "The *internally moving* forces of matter as *machine,* that is, as a body that has *internally moving* force according to the laws of mechanics, yields the a priori concept of an organic body whose parts, connected in one system, move each other in accordance with specific laws" (21:197.11–15). Moreover, Kant insists, we are ourselves the prime example of such a purposive organization: "Because man is conscious of himself as a self-moving machine . . . he can, and is entitled to, introduce a priori organic-moving forces of bodies into the classification of bodies in general—although only indirectly, according to the analogy with the moving force of a body as a machine" (21:213, Op. 66). In other words, we must generalize the concept of our own "self-moving machine" and be open to the possibility that we might encounter in experience other natural machines, that is, living organisms.

This circumstance, too, seems to speak against Mathieu's thesis which I mentioned at the beginning, namely, that it was Kant's dissatisfaction with the third *Critique* that convinced him that a "science of transition" was required. The inclusion of organisms and natural machines into the program of the Transition can be explained entirely internally, as following naturally from Kant's discussion of the ponderability of matter, and of the mechanical powers.

If one thinks an external stimulus is needed to explain this shift in Kant's train of thought, one should perhaps again look at Gehler's *Physicalisches Wörterbuch.* In the article titled "Physischer Hebel" (Physical Lever), Gehler points out that "even the muscles of the animal body, when moving its limbs, act in accordance with the law of the lever."[24] And here too he draws on Kästner as his authority. But to insist that Kant was influenced on this point by Gehler or Kästner would be mere speculation.

The "Green Color of a Lawn" and Kant's Theory of Matter

Vittorio Mathieu was not the first to have linked Kant's last work with the *Critique of Judgment*. In 1938, the editor of the *Opus postumum* in the Academy edition, Gerhard Lehmann, wrote in his Introduction: "When Kant again took up problems of physics, we may presume that he connected the schema of a transition from the *Critique of Judgment* with the requirement of a realization of transcendental philosophy from the *Metaphysical Foundations of Natural Science*. From this he gained the conception of a new science of a transition" (22:752).

One year later, in his *Habilitationsschrift*,[1] Lehmann developed his thesis of the origin of the *Opus postumum* in Kant's third *Critique* in greater detail. The *Metaphysical Foundations* suddenly receded entirely into the background. After a brief reference to it in the Introduction, Lehmann did not mention it again. Although, as he admitted, "there are no direct references to the *Critique of Judgment* in Kant's *Opus postumum*," he nevertheless found enough "indirect" evidence to feel compelled to claim: "The internal development of the *Opus postumum* suggests the question whether the *origin* of the entire work is not also related to the *Critique of Judgment*. This is indeed the case."[2] And he concluded his study with the claim: "None [*sic*] of the problems [of the *Opus postumum*] . . . can be comprehended and interpreted without the *Critique of Judgment*."[3]

Lehmann subsequently reiterated his position in numerous publications, and influential commentators, including the editors of the Italian (Vittorio Mathieu), Spanish (Felix Duque), and French (François Marty) editions of Kant's *Opus postumum,* have endorsed his view. Mathieu's own *La filosofia trascendentale e l'OP di Kant* of 1958 was the first systematic study of the *Opus postumum* after its publication in the Academy edition, setting the stage for subsequent interpretations, especially in Italy. In 1989 Mathieu published another book on the *Opus postumum,* this time in German, which represents the fruits of his lifelong reflections on Kant's last work.[4]

Although they both believe in the origin of Kant's Transition project in the *Critique of Judgment,* neither Lehmann nor Mathieu discusses the early fascicles of the *Opus postumum* in relation to the third *Critique.* In order to establish their thesis, they tend to concentrate on the latter parts of Kant's last work—those written in 1799 and later. At this time Kant began to include the concept of organic forces, of natural purposes or natural machines, in the program of the Transition. In all previous drafts he had insisted that the distinction between organic and inorganic bodies belongs to physics: to treat of it in the transition to physics would be a *metabasis eis allo genos,* an illegitimate transgression into the domain of the *empirical* science of nature. Yet Kant abandoned this view in 1799, a change both Lehmann and Mathieu attribute to the need for a third edition of the *Critique of Judgment* in the same year. Lehmann writes—and Mathieu quotes him approvingly on this point— that "the task to prepare a new edition of the third *Critique*" was the "*causa occasionalis*" for Kant's renewed occupation with this work.[5] "One can hardly deny," Lehmann adds, "that the inclusion of biological-teleological problems in Kant's last work is connected with the publication of the third edition of the third *Critique*."

On the contrary, I think that one can, indeed, that one has good reasons to deny this claim. First, it is far from certain that Kant was at all involved with the preparation of the third edition of the *Critique of Judgment*—any more than with the second edition, which was in all likelihood prepared for publication by Friedrich Gentz, a former student of Kant's,[6] or even the first edition, which was prepared by Kiesewetter. Second, Kant's publisher, F. T. Lagarde, had already sent the honorarium for the third edition to Kant on August 4, 1798 (see 12:248 and 13:484f.), whereas the problem of living organisms is not discussed in the Transition until half a year later. Finally, as we saw in the previous chapter, the inclusion of organic forces in the Transition project can be explained entirely internally, from Kant's discussion of the ponderability of matter and of the mechanical powers.

Rather than marking a return to his earlier work, the inclusion of natural purposes in the Transition indicates how far, by 1799, Kant had in fact moved beyond the third *Critique*. Amidst the detailed discussion of living organisms in the Critique of Teleological Judgment, the unique organism that is one's own body had remained conspicuously absent.[7] This absence was for a reason. Kant had initially intended to write only a "critique of taste" (10:515). In the course of carrying out this task, however, he became convinced that it would be appropriate to expand the project so as to include a critique of teleological judgment as well, since both types of judgment, aesthetic as well as teleological, belong to the same faculty, namely, the power of reflective judgment (see the First Introduction, 20:244).

Nevertheless, Kant thought that there is a fundamental difference between aesthetic and teleological judgments. The experience of beauty is such that an otherwise unknown harmonious play of the cognitive faculties *can be sensed* in the form of pleasure—a feeling that, because it concerns nothing but a formal relation of our cognitive faculties, can and must be presupposed in everyone who perceives the same object. And it is this sensation, this subjective yet generalizable *experience,* according to Kant, that demonstrates to us that nature not only harmonizes in its transcendental laws with our understanding but also, in its empirical laws, it harmonizes necessarily with judgment and its ability to exhibit nature (20:233).

There is, Kant thought, no corresponding sensation in the experience of purposive products of nature, of living organisms. Whereas the aesthetic estimation of natural beauty discovers a purposiveness of nature *for the subject,* any purposiveness *in the object* is completely "beyond" (20:233) the power of judgment: "What is more, even experience cannot prove the actuality of such purposes" (5:359). Because Kant here contrasts natural purposes with human artifacts, whose designer is always external to them, he concludes that the self-organization of nature has nothing analogous to any causality known to us. We can never know from experience whether an object of outer sense is indeed a natural purpose, although we may have good reasons to reflect on it as if it were (cf. 5:§65).

In the relevant passages of the *Opus postumum,* and as a result of Kant's reflections on mechanical powers and on the ponderability of matter, this position is modified. It is *through experience,* indeed, that we have the concept of a natural purpose, but it is not the human artifact and the realization of practical purposes that originally permits the formation of this concept. Rather it is the experience of our own bodily organization, of our body's ability to exercise intentionally moving forces in accordance with the laws of mechanics: "Because man is conscious of himself as a self-moving machine . . . he can, and is entitled to, introduce a priori organic-moving forces of bodies into the classification of bodies in general" (21:213, Op. 66). In a later passage from the tenth fascicle, Kant describes this newly gained insight in the following way: "We experience organic forces in our own body; and we come, by means of the analogy with them (with a part of their principle) to the concept of a vegetative body, leaving out the animal part of its principle" (22:373, Op. 118; cf. 22:383, Op. 120). Our own bodily experience functions as the paradigm for the estimation of other objects as organic; it is the primary example by which we judge all others. But as a paradigm for natural purposiveness, it cannot be subject to the 'as if' principle of the third *Critique:* this principle fails to hold in the case of our own bodily organization.[8] My body thus plays a unique role in my relation to the world around me—a role Kant will explore in subsequent fascicles, in connection with the doctrine of self-positing. But even in the present drafts, the contrast with the "distant analogy" (5:375) between natural purposes and human artifacts that lies at the foundation of the Critique of Teleological Judgment could hardly be greater.

Although I cannot agree with Lehmann and Mathieu's thesis about the origin of the *Opus postumum* in Kant's third *Critique,* I want to look at another possible connection between these two works, one that has so far been ignored by all commentators. And yet, if the connection obtained, it would point up the impact the *Opus postumum* had on the third edition of the *Critique of Judgment,* not the other way around. For in the 1799 edition of that work, we encounter a remarkable correction of the two earlier editions—a correction which, if made by Kant, can be explained only with reference to the intervening development of his thoughts in the *Opus postumum*. At least this is how it seems to me.

The passage I have in mind occurs not in the Critique of Teleological Judgment but in the Critique of Aesthetic Judgment. There, in §§14 and 51, Kant considers the question whether a mere color (such as the green color of a lawn) or a mere tone (for example, that of a violin) could be called beautiful. Since he argues that a judgment of taste is to be based on nothing but the *form of purposiveness* of an object (§11), whereas colors and tones seem to depend only on sensation, that is, the matter of the representation, the answer, it appears, must be negative. Moreover, the delight we might take in a color or a tone does not seem to admit of universal agreement, for we cannot assume that in all subjects the sensations agree in quality. Hence, one might argue, colors and tones deserve only to be called agreeable, not beautiful. But, Kant continues, and it is this passage that will be revised in the third edition:

> If, following Euler, we assume that colors are vibrations of the ether in uniform temporal sequence, as, in the case of sounds, tones are such vibrations of the air, and if we assume—what is most important (but which I doubt very much)—that the mind perceives not only, by sense, the effect that these vibrations have on the excitement of the organ, but also, by reflection, the regular play of the impressions (and hence the form in the connection of different representations), then color and tone would not be mere sensations but would already be the formal determination of the manifold in these, in which case they could even by themselves be considered beauties. (5:224)

In the third edition of the *Critique of Judgment,* the phrase "but which I doubt very much"—namely, that by reflection the mind perceives the regular play of the impressions—is replaced with "which, after all, I do not doubt at all."[9] Although we do not know for certain, it is difficult to imagine that anyone but Kant himself could be responsible for such a significant alteration of the text. But why?

First, we should note that Kant does not doubt that tones are vibrations of the air: "Tones are such vibrations of the air," he states explicitly. He is less certain, it seems, whether colors are vibrations of the ether. This was indeed the view of Leonhard Euler. Euler held that light and sound are strictly analogous phenomena, whose differences consist only in differences of frequency and the speed of propagation. In §22 of his *Nova theoria lucis et colorum,* for example, Euler wrote: "I maintain that light above all travels through an as it were elastic medium, by means of pulsation, in a manner similar to sound; and just as sound travels mostly through the air, so I take it that light travels through a different as it were elastic medium, which fills not only our atmosphere, but also the entire cosmic space between us and the most distant fixed stars."[10] But second, and more important, Kant seems more inclined in the case of tones than in the case of colors to think that the mind perceives by reflection the regular play of the impressions. This is at least suggested by §51, where Kant explicitly states that he did declare music to be the beautiful play of sensations (5:325). To this one might object that music is not a mere tone but a regular play of them, and hence can be called beautiful even though a single tone cannot. But this would be too simplistic a response. For in this section, Kant discusses "music" and the "art of color" together as the two possible candidates of an "art of the beautiful play of sensations." Yet at the end he claims only that music can be beautiful; he does not make a corresponding claim for the "art of color." Why should a rainbow (or a drawing of it) not be entitled to the attribute "beautiful" if a musical scale is?

The problem Kant is struggling with here is due, it seems, to the fact that from the aesthetic point of view, a mere tone and a mere color are strictly parallel phenomena, whereas from a physical point of view they might not be. More precisely, singular tones and colors are only agreeable rather than beautiful unless the mind perceives by reflection the regular play of the impressions—that is to say, if we can come to know the mathematical character of the proportions of the vibrations of their respective media. For we do not have to be sensibly aware of them, and we certainly are not sensibly aware of the proportions of the vibrations of the air in the case of music. It is for good reasons that Kant says that the mind must perceive *by reflection* the regular play of the impressions. And the reflection concerns the mathematical form of the vibrations of the elastic medium. Thus Kant writes in §53 of the third *Critique:* "Although this mathematical form is not represented by means of determinate concepts, to it alone belongs the delight which the mere reflection upon such a number of concomitant or consecutive sensations couples with this their play, as the universally valid condition of its beauty, and it is with reference to it alone that taste can lay claim to a right to anticipate the judgment of everyone" (5:329).

What is true of concomitant or consecutive tones must also be true of single tones, for these, too, depend on "the numerical relation of the vibration of the air in the same time" (5:329). Thus the problem comes down to the following: like single tones, single colors can be said to be beautiful "if, following Euler, we [can] assume that colors are vibrations of the ether in uniform temporal sequence." Whether this is the case, however, was not at all clear to Kant in 1790.

In the *Metaphysical Foundations of Natural Science,* which was written in 1785 and published in the following year, Kant had noted that Euler's wave theory of light has great "difficulty in making the rectilinear motion of the light conceivable," although he pointed out that this difficulty is due to an unduly "mathematical"—that is, mechanical—representation of the ether as an aggregation of particles. This difficulty could be avoided by representing the ether dynamically, "as originally and indeed thoroughly fluid" (4:520). Euler, who followed Descartes in his theory of the ether, thought of it as an exceedingly fine and elastic medium consisting of infinitely many minute particles whose fundamental property was impenetrability. "Light," he wrote to Frederike Charlotte von Brandenburg Schwedt in the twentieth of his *Letters to a German Princess on Various Objects of Physics and Philosophy*, "is nothing other than a motion or vibration in the smallest *parts* of the ether." That Kant was at this time reluctant to endorse Euler's theory is also clear from the so-called *Danziger Physik* of the same year (summer semester 1785), where Kant maintained that Euler's theory had not yet been established with sufficient certainty (29:150–154).

But what is important about Kant's remark concerning Euler is that although he knows that a dynamical theory of the ether is preferable to a mechanical one, he does not endorse either.[11] In fact, in 1785 Kant is not committed to any theory of the ether, nor is he in 1790. The matter theory of the *Metaphysical Foundations of Natural Science* does not require an ether, and Kant had not abandoned this theory when he published the *Critique of Judgment*. A year later, in a draft of a letter to Christoph Friedrich Hellwag, Kant speaks again of his "comparison between colors and tones in an aesthetic judgment," but points out that in the third *Critique* he had presented this comparison merely "as a problem," and that he has not yet arrived at a solution to this problem (13:294). Another two years later, in 1793, a second edition of the *Critique of Judgment* came out. Kant still had not changed his mind, although by this time he has serious doubts about the theory of matter presented in the *Metaphysical Foundations*. This can be witnessed in a letter by Kant of October 16, 1792, to his former pupil, the mathematician Jacob Sigismund Beck.

[32]

⁓◊⁓

In 1791 Beck had accepted an offer from Kant to write *Erläuternde Auszüge*—explanatory excerpts—of Kant's major writings. Kant's hope was that Beck, "because of the decidedness and clarity which you as a mathematician can lend your discourse also in the field of metaphysics" (11:256), would make his philosophy more accessible to the general reader and counter some of the criticisms that had been leveled against it. To this end he offered to answer any queries or doubts Beck might have. As a result, a highly instructive correspondence ensued between them in which Beck elicited often detailed comments from his former teacher.

From the start, Beck conceived of his project in three volumes. The third he set aside to answer critics, and to present Kant's philosophy from his own "standpoint."[12] The other two volumes were dedicated to the exposition of Kant's major writings. The first volume explicated Kant's critiques of pure and practical reason; the second was intended to do the same for the *Metaphysical Foundations of Natural Science* and the *Critique of Judgment*. The fact that Beck regarded the *Metaphysical Foundations* as important enough to treat it as extensively in his presentation as the three *Critiques* was especially welcome to Kant, for unlike his other writings, this work had so far failed to receive the attention he had hoped for.

In a letter of September 8, 1792, Beck inquired how precisely he might understand the differences of density in matter on the basis of Kant's dynamical theory, and offered an explanation of his own. Kant covered the letter with extensive reflections on this problem (11:361–365). In his answer of October 16, he wrote, after acknowledging the importance of the question: "I would expect a solution to this problem in the following: that attraction (the universal, Newtonian) is originally the same in all matter, and only the repulsion of different [types of matter] is different and thus accounts for the specific differences of their density. But this leads in a way into a circle that I cannot get out of, and about which I still have to try to come to a better understanding" (11:376f.).

It is not immediately obvious how to assess Kant's own diagnosis. Is his explanation really circular? And if so, why? What does the circle consist in? A survey of the very sparse literature on this topic provides hardly any help at all.[13] In trying to shed light on Kant's remark, I will approach it in a somewhat roundabout way, and from a number of different angles.

1. What is the alleged nature of the circle from Kant's point of view? Let us begin by noticing that the explanation of differences in density stated in the letter to Beck is the same Kant gave in the *Metaphysical Foundations*. All matter, so he had argued there, is possible only by the interplay of two conflicting forces, repulsion and attraction. Space can be filled in a determined measure only by the "action and reaction of both fundamental forces" (4:521): inasmuch as the repulsion increases in greater measure upon approach of the parts of matter than the attraction does, a point of equilibrium will be reached which determines the limit of approach beyond which, by means of the given attraction, no greater is possible, and hence also the degree of compression that constitutes the measure of the filling of space.

Differences in density are possible because the relation of both forces can vary infinitely. The repulsive force acts only at the surface of contact, it being "all the same whether behind this surface much or little . . . matter is found" (4:524). It may thus be originally different in degree in different types of matter. The attractive force, by contrast, goes beyond the surface and acts directly on all parts of a matter. As a penetrative force it is always proportional to the quantity of matter (4:516). The degree of the filling of space can thus vary according to their measures.

Now, it is noteworthy that Kant, in the letter to Beck, explicitly identifies the force of attraction with Newtonian grav-

THE "GREEN COLOR OF A LAWN" AND KANT'S THEORY OF MATTER

itation. In the *Metaphysical Foundations* he pointed out that the attractive force, making possible "the thing which fills a space in a determinate degree," also makes possible the physical contact of matter. Its action must consequently be prior to, and independent of, the condition of contact. Hence, it must be "an immediate action through empty space of one matter upon another" (4:512, Proposition 7 and Proof). Such an action is known as Newtonian attraction, or gravitation.

This identification, however, introduces a serious problem into Kant's theory. For gravitational attraction is always proportional to the mass or, for a given volume, the density of a matter (4:514.33–35, 516.20). So the intensity of the attractive force must causally depend on density, and density must in turn be the effect of attraction—an explanation that he now, in 1792, regarded as circular. In addition, this explanation appears to be in conflict with Kant's original assumption that a determinate degree of density results from the interplay of *both,* attraction and repulsion. It is precisely these problems that Kant mentions at the opening of the extended notes he scribbled on Beck's letter to him:

> The greatest difficulty is to explain how a determinate volume of matter is possible through the attraction of its own part[s] according to the inverse square of the distance, together with [*bey*] a repulsion that can only extend to the immediately contacting parts (not those at a distance) according to the cube of the distance (hence the volume itself). *For the power to attract depends on the density [of this matter], this density in turn on the power to attract.* Also, the density depends on [*sich richten nach*] the inverse relation of repulsion, i.e. the volume. (11:361f.; my italics)

2. Assuming that we have correctly identified the circle that Kant saw in his theory of matter, what are we to make of

it? A likely response might be that not every instance of reciprocal causal dependence must be circular. Here examples from contemporary physics readily come to mind. For instance, the charge distribution of the electrons in the shells of an atom is generated by the electromagnetic potential present there; the same electromagnetic potential in turn is generated by the charge distribution of the electrons. Nevertheless, this reciprocal dependence is not circular because a unique value can be determined for the two quantities involved, by a method of reciprocal adaptation.[14] This presupposes, however, the availability of at least two independent laws or hypotheses (in this case, the Schrödinger equation and Maxwell's equations) that relate the two quantities to each other. These relations can then be subjected to a procedure of successive approximation by reciprocal adaptation until a self-consistent result is achieved. The interdependence in question is thus non-circular.

But examples of this type are of limited value for the assessment of Kant's position, even if they are instructive in their own right. They are of limited value not so much because Kant, it goes without saying, did not have available to him the tools of contemporary physics. Nor is it per se crucial that Kant has available not two but only one independent law to relate both, density and the intensity of attraction, thus making impossible the kind of reciprocal adaptation described above. Within a contemporary framework, this would mean only that no unique values can be determined for the two relata on the basis of Kant's own theory, which need not be regarded as a serious problem. It becomes a crucial point, in my view, only if we realize that Kant is concerned primarily not with physical theories of particular entities but with the metaphysical principles of the *construction* of the concept of "a something that is to be an object of the external senses" (4:476), that is, matter. This is borne out even by the first sentence, quoted above, from Kant's notes on Beck's letter, to wit, the sentence immediately preceding the statement of circularity: it connects directly with Kant's explication of such a construction at 4:521.4–8. The question of circularity thus has to be addressed first of all with regard to the constructibility of the concept of matter, and it is only then, I suggest, that we will see the deeper and more serious problem for Kant's theory arise. This will be the topic of the next chapter. For now it must suffice to note that Kant himself was in no doubt about the circularity in his account; he also knew where to look for a possible solution to his problem. A clear trace of this can be found on "Loses Blatt 38," an early leaf of the *Opus postumum* which Adickes dated "from the second half of the '80s,"[15] but which we can now more confidently bring into proximity with the letter to Beck: "The question is whether apart from universal attraction there be another one which acts originally, according to different laws?" (21:430.10–12).

⸻◦⸻

Before turning to Kant's attempts to deal with the circularity in his theory of matter, let us look briefly at some contemporary responses to the *Metaphysical Foundations*.

1. Nine years after its publication, in a letter to Kant, Kiesewetter noted the "peculiar fact" that so far only "very few people" had concerned themselves with this work (12:23). Indeed, few reviews had greeted its publication.[16] And these, for the most part, simply summarized its four chapters. In the few cases in which reservations were expressed, however, they concentrated on Kant's assumption of repulsion as an essential force of matter. For example, an early review published anonymously in the *Göttingischen Anzeigen von gelehrten Sachen* (1786), but penned by Abraham Kästner, asked doubtfully with regard to Kant's claim that matter fills a space not by its

mere existence but only by a repulsive force: "*Must* one think of a moving force in a wall, because, at the wall, one cannot progress further?"[17] A few years later, Tobias Mayer examined Kant's theory in an article "Ob es nöthig sey, eine zurück-stoßende Kraft in der Natur anzunehmen" (Whether It Be Necessary to Assume a Repulsive Force in Nature), a question he decidedly answered in the negative.[18] J. S. T. Gehler endorsed Mayer's view in his influential *Physicalisches Wörter-buch* (1787–1795), the scientific encyclopedia Kant frequently used while working on the *Opus postumum*. Gehler regarded it as a fact that Tobias Mayer had demonstrated the untenability of all known proofs for the existence of original repulsive forces (see Op. 260–261, notes 22–23). Kant excerpted these texts, but his conviction that two conflicting forces are required for the possibility of matter was not shaken thereby; it had stood firm at least since his *Monadologia physica* of 1756 (see 1:476).

2. A comparison of Kant's *Metaphysical Foundations* with other theories of matter prevalent at his time shows that his theory was not unique in that it evoked both attractive and repulsive forces. Rather, it is the supposed interaction of these two forces that makes his theory unique.[19] R. G. Boscovich, for example, also worked with the two forces of attraction and repulsion, which he, like Kant, located in the same material particles. Unlike Kant, however, he assumed that these forces *alternate* in their activity. For Boscovich, a particle can exert no repulsive force unless its attractive force has previously decreased to zero, and vice versa. By contrast, Herman Boerhaave worked with a conflict model like Kant's, but he located the two conflicting forces in two different types of matter: the particles of the heat-material or caloric *(Wärmestoff)* exert repulsive force, whereas regular material particles exert attractive force; these two forces do not alternate their influence but act in opposition to each other. Kant's position in the *Metaphysical Foundations* seems

to be unique in that he works with conflicting (not alternating) forces located in the same parts of matter. That such a theory is not without problems Kant was aware of even at the time of writing (see 4:518–523).

3. Kant's theory of matter was also criticized for evoking *too few* forces, a criticism expressed first by Franz von Baader[20] and subsequently, and more forcefully, by the young Schelling. In 1797, in his *Ideas for a Philosophy of Nature,* Schelling had still endorsed the Kantian theory, but for the second, revised edition of the text he added a critical supplement to the fifth chapter of Book 2 ("Basic Principles of Dynamics"). His earlier account had shared in the "defectiveness" of the Kantian theory, he now explained, in that the necessity of a *third* principle of the construction of matter had eluded it: "That the attractive force is equated to the force of gravity and conversely is merely a consequence of that . . . defect."[21]

Schelling developed his own position in particular in the "First Draft of a Philosophy of Nature" (1799) and in the "Universal Deduction of the Dynamical Process" (1800). According to these works, in the *Metaphysical Foundations,* Kant conflates two different strategies, namely, the analysis of matter as a given, or as a "product" in space, with the genetic account of the production of matter as an object of experience. In other words, Kant analyzes the "product" matter with regard to its dynamical properties, then uses the result of this analysis to explain how matter is possible.

Schelling's objection amounts to this: if we start with the given *product*—the empirical concept of matter—we can indeed deduce analytically the two conflicting forces of repulsion and attraction from the fact that this matter fills a space by a determinate degree. But if we want to explain the *production* of matter from these two forces, the explanation will perforce be circular, for a third force is needed for its production. If two forces *seem* to suffice, then matter has already secretly been presupposed in the explanation—"a confusion of which quite a few traces can be met with for example in Kant's Dynamics."[22] According to Schelling, when Kant explains how matter first becomes possible through the interplay of two fundamental forces, he already thinks of these forces as conjoined with matter qua product. Thus, with regard to Kant's characterization of attraction and repulsion as penetrative and contact forces, respectively, Schelling asks: "How can one think of contact except where there is already impenetrability, i.e., matter, and how of penetration without something penetrable?"[23] It is because of this ambiguity, Schelling thinks, that Kant equates the attractive force required to limit the expansive force of repulsion with gravitational attraction. But the attractive force was introduced to explain how the original expansive force receives finitude and determinateness. From the point of view of the formation or production of matter, the attractive force required to balance the repulsive force is absorbed by, or "exhausted" *(erschöpft)* in, this production: "What Kant calls attraction . . . is an altogether *intransitive* force—a force that is used only for the construction of the individual products, and that exhausts itself in this construction. The force of gravity, by contrast, is a *transitive* force, that is, a force with which the product is supposed to act *beyond* itself."[24]

To fill a determinate space, the repulsive force has to be limited to a certain degree. For this limitation, attraction is required, yet not attraction in general but a force that is itself limited to a certain degree. What determines the degree of *its* limitation, and hence the degree of both, Schelling thinks, must be a ground lying outside the two forces considered in themselves:

> The empirical datum that belongs to the construction of a body with a determinate degree of the filling of space is thus that the degree of its attractive

force must previously [*zum voraus*] be limited and determined by *bodies outside it.* Since this relation must be reciprocal in such a way that the attractive force of each body is limited to a certain degree by that of every other body, one can see that the empirical datum required for the construction of a determinate degree of the filling of space is the universal concatenation [*Verkettung*] of all matter among itself.[25]

It is unlikely that Schelling had any detailed knowledge of Kant's work on the *Opus postumum;* to what extent Kant took notice of Schelling's writings is still unclear.[26] At any rate, Kant seems to have found a solution for his problem several years before Schelling's texts were published—moreover, one quite different from Schelling's solution. Nevertheless, it may be helpful to view Kant's own development against the objections of his younger disciple.

First, it is noteworthy that in the *Metaphysical Foundations,* after establishing that attraction is the second force necessary to fill a space in a determinate manner, Kant expresses uncertainty as to whether the mutual attraction of the *parts* of the matter compressed in that space is sufficient for the task, or whether the influence of matter external to it is also needed. In note 2 to the proof of Proposition 8, he writes: "It may be that the attraction involved in this determinate degree of the filling of space arises from the individual attraction of the parts of the compressed matter among one another or arises from the union of this compressed matter with the attraction of all the matter of the world" (4:518). If we turn to the extensive notes that he scribbled on Beck's letter to him of September 8, 1792, we find that Kant now favors the latter option: "In order to explain the difference in density, one has to assume that one and the same attractive force of a given quantity of matter acts against an infinitely varied repulsive force, but that it could not counterbalance the latter . . . except through the attraction of the entire universe" (11: 362.28–33; see also 364.23–26, 365.25–28, 365.34–37; with one exception: 365.1–2). Yet by this he can hardly mean the gravitational attraction exerted by other material bodies (terrestrial or celestial), as for them the same problem would arise with regard to *their* possibility. An alternative account, however, is not yet in sight. I take this to be the reason why Kant, in his answer to Beck of a few weeks later, still acknowledges that his explanation of the differences in density in terms of originally different degrees of repulsion and "the universal, Newtonian" attraction leads into a circle that he cannot get out of.

There is, however, among Kant's notes on the Beck letter, also one that considers the possible formation of "persisting lumps" *(beharrliche Klumpen)* of matter from the "concussions" of a "certain original thinness of the universe" (11: 362.13–16). This idea, which is mentioned rather in passing, bears an interesting resemblance to an earlier *Reflexion* (no. 44) of Kant's from around 1775–1777. There Kant had assumed two entirely different types of attraction: "All kinds of matter can be regarded as so many different attracting points, but of varying degrees, according to whose measure the mass of the matter is a densified ether. Thus the ether is not a particular kind of matter, as far as impenetrability is concerned, but all types of matter consist of ether, which is attracted in various degrees. This attraction is not gravitational attraction but one that checks [*hemmt*] the tremblings of the ether" (14:334–336).

Kant here distinguishes between an original attraction that commences from attracting points of differing degree and intensity, and gravitational attraction. The former restrains the expansive force of the ether (its tremblings), thereby condensing it into material entities of varying masses; the latter is proportional to these masses and thus a secondary attraction.

Any differences in density and mass in different types of matter thus depend, in this account, on the degree to which ether has been condensed in a given space.

This view is not compatible with the theory of the *Metaphysical Foundations*. Among other things, by 1786 Kant had replaced the dynamical monadology of originally attracting points underlying *Reflexion* 44 with a theory of matter as a continuous quantity that is infinitely divisible and that has no smallest "parts." And in his notes on the letter from Beck, Kant indeed only considers the oscillations of the "original thinness of the universe" as a possible explanation of the *cohesion* of matter (attraction in contact, not in distance), which, as he realizes, can just as little be explained as the effect of the attraction of the parts of a matter as can the differences in density.

Nevertheless, it is not difficult to imagine how Kant's thoughts must have progressed from here. To resolve the circle in his dynamical theory of matter, different types or manifestations of attraction have to be considered. More precisely, the "fundamental determination of a something that is to be an object of the external senses" (4:476) that Kant had begun in the *Metaphysical Foundations* needs to take into account cohesion as well as gravitational attraction. Kant did this on various loose leaves which now constitute the earliest part of the *Opus postumum*. They lead to the result that cohesion is possible only through the living force (impact) of a matter outside it, that is, the ether (see, e.g., 21:454, Op. 5, and so on). With this result established, Kant composed the first systematic draft of his last work, the *Oktaventwurf* of 1796. It contains the first clear statement of the theory of matter of the *Opus postumum*, a theory that from now on undergoes only minor variations:

> An inwardly merely expansive (aerial) matter is so
> either *originally (originarie expansiva)* or only de-

rivatively *(deritative expansiva)*. One could call the former the ether, but not as an object of experience; rather, merely as the idea of an expansive matter whose parts are not capable of any greater dissolution, because no attraction of cohesion can be found in them . . . All matter, however, is originally combined in a whole of world-attraction through universal gravitation, and thus the ether itself would, however far it may extend, be in a state of compression, even in the absence of all other matter. Such compression must, however, be oscillating, because the first effect of this attraction in the beginning of all things must be a compression of all its parts toward some midpoint, with consequential expansion, and which, because of the elasticity [of the world-matter], must hence be set in continuous and everlasting oscillation. The secondary matter distributed in the ether is thereby necessitated to unify itself into bodies at certain points and so to form cosmic bodies. This universal attraction, which the matter of the ether exerts upon itself, must be thought of as a limited space (a sphere), consequently as the one universal cosmic body, which compresses itself in a certain degree through this attraction. It must, however, be regarded, just in virtue of this original compression and expansion, as eternally oscillating, and hence, all cohesion can only have been produced (or be produced further) by the living force of impact, not the dead force of pressure. (21:378f., Op. 12)

Thus Kant now distinguishes between the attraction and repulsion of an ether in which all secondary matter was originally dissolved, and the attraction and repulsion required to fill a space in determinate measure. With this, we can return to the question of a circle in Kant's argument. In the *Opus postumum*, Kant preserves the insight that repulsion is an essential force of matter. To counterbalance its original expansion, and hence to fill a space to a determinate degree, attraction is indeed required, but not the universal, penetrative force of attraction (gravitation), but attraction in contact, or cohesion (see, e.g., 21:387, Op. 13; 21:409, Op. 20; 22:215, Op. 33). Since cohesion is a contact force, its measure does not depend on the quantity of a given matter. This is the first step in avoiding the circle. The second step consists in showing that cohesion itself—indeed all internally moving forces of matter—depends on the living force of an ether (21:374, Op. 10; see also 22:264.4, 267.8, and so on). The quantity of matter, and the differences in density, is thus a function of this universally distributed *Weltstoff* whose internal pulsations segregate *(entmischen)* the heterogeneous materials originally dissolved in it, thereby causing the formation of bodies of different types and textures. In the ether's own unceasing pulsations or oscillations, however, attraction and repulsion *alternate* (see, e.g., 21:310, Op. 25; 21:312, Op. 26; 22:211, Op. 31; 21:181, Op. 58; and so on).

We can now, finally, return to the discussion of the third *Critique*. What is important in the present context, and what marks a decisive change with regard to the *Metaphysical Foundations*, is Kant's new conviction that any matter of a particular form, hence any physical *body*, is conceivable only on the basis of a universally distributed, oscillating ether. From the perspective of the *Oktaventwurf* of 1796, it can no longer be maintained that the *Metaphysical Foundations* contains a "doctrine of body" (4:470, 473, 477, 478, and so on); it only formulates a theory of matter in general. Nor can it be maintained any longer that cohesion is merely a physical, not a metaphysical, property (4:518)—it is required for any matter of a certain form, hence for any object of outer sense. Thus Kant writes in the *Oktaventwurf*: "Cohesion is thus the first thing ... which requires explanation, and original difference of density, which arises therefrom [as] its consequence ... To assume such a matter [i.e., ether] filling cosmic space is an inevitably necessary hypothesis, for, without it, no cohesion, which is necessary for the formation of a physical *body*, can be thought" (21:374–378, Op. 10–12). By 1796, then, Kant was himself committed to the assumption of a dynamical ether, on the basis of his own theory of matter. It would not be surprising if he took the first opportunity to make the required change in the *Critique of Judgment*, and replace the phrase "which I doubt very much" with "which, after all, I do not doubt at all." Remember that the passage in which this phrase occurs asks only that, "following Euler, we assume that colors are vibrations of the ether in uniform temporal sequence." It is not that we are to adopt Euler's mechanical model of the ether.

Moreover, a brief survey of the *Opus postumum* reveals that Euler's theory of light and the analogy between colors and tones are still very much on Kant's mind (although his views on this topic did not acquire complete consistency). Even before 1796, Kant had adopted a modified undulation theory of light. On Loose Leaf 24, probably written the year before the *Oktaventwurf*, Kant notes: "Light is the effect of the pulsating ether, which vibrates from every point in all directions and, as such, in no straight line" (21:469.4–6; see also 21:387, Op. 13). The ether "as such" vibrates in no straight line. Pulsations, however, are of "two different kinds," those that propagate "in straight lines" (light), and those that propagate "in all directions" (21:503.24–25). And because the ether of the *Opus postumum*, unlike Euler's, is thoroughly dynamical and *stratified* (22:106.26), Kant thinks it can make intelligible what seems to be the main stumbling block for Euler's mechanical theory—the rectilinear motion of light: "The ether which, as stratified, either according to its condensation [*Verdichtung*] or its heterogeneity, acts through light . . . This ether, moving as elastic matter in straight lines, would be called light-material; when absorbed by bodies, and expanding them, it would be called caloric" (22:111.13–14, 214, Op. 33). The concept of a pulsating ether thus has to be brought to bear on the phenomenon of heat as well: "Euler's pulsations of the ether are to be applied here not just to light but also to the motion of heat" (21:523, Op. 35).

Finally, Kant points out at various places that the motion of light admits of a purely mathematical treatment, analogous to that of the motion of sound. The concept of a repulsive force, he writes in one such passage, "which extends itself in cosmic space . . . by means of light and its law of motion in colors . . . is thoroughly mathematical" (22:517.11–14). In other words, Kant now "does not doubt at all" that colors are vibrations of the ether in uniform temporal sequence, and that the mind, by reflection, can "perceive the regular play of the impressions." Hence, a mere color, just as much as a singular tone, may justifiably be called "beautiful."

CHAPTER THREE

The "Gap" in Kant's
Critical Philosophy

Kant did not make it easy for his interpreters; few problems in his work, however, have left the sympathetic reader quite as puzzled as his remark, made repeatedly in 1798, that there is "a gap" in his critical philosophy. In a letter to Christian Garve of September 21 of that year, for instance, Kant reports "a pain like that of Tantalus" of seeing before him "the unpaid bill of my uncompleted philosophy." There still remains "a gap" in the system of critical philosophy, he writes, which reason demands be filled (12:257). Of this "gap" Kant also writes a month later to Kiesewetter. Informing his former pupil of the work he is currently engaged in, Kant explains: "With that work the task of the critical philosophy will be completed and a gap that now stands open will be filled" (12:258).

These remarks have puzzled commentators ever since, for Kant had completed the *critical* philosophy eight years earlier, with the publication of the *Critique of Judgment.* And he had completed it to his own satisfaction, as seems clear from the Preface to that work, where he announced: "With this, then, I bring my entire critical undertaking to a close. I shall hasten to the doctrinal part" (5:170). This doctrinal part is of course the often promised system of metaphysics in accordance with the critical standards, for which the three *Critiques* had merely been the groundwork, the "propaedeutic" (A841).

But what makes Kant's remarks in his letters to Garve and Kiesewetter particularly puzzling is the special nature of the project from which he expected the completion of his critical work. The project, he explained, consists in "the transition from the metaphysical foundations of natural science to physics" (12:257, 258). When Kant had published his *Metaphysical Foundations of Natural Science* twelve years earlier, he had also included in its Preface a statement of completion and closure: "I believe that I have completely exhausted this metaphysical doctrine of body,[1] as far as such a doctrine ever extends . . . There is no more to do in the way of discovery or addition" (4:473, 476). Yet even if, for the reasons discussed in the previous chapters, he had changed his mind on this point during the intervening years, what bearing could a "transition" from metaphysics to an empirical science such as physics possibly have on Kant's *critical* system? Where is the gap?

It is no exaggeration to say that Kant scholars have as yet failed to come to terms with this paradoxical situation, and consequently have failed to understand fully the nature of Kant's last work. Early generations assumed an onset of senility on Kant's part, and a failure of memory regarding what he had written a decade earlier. Kuno Fischer, most notorious of them all, complained that we get to see "neither the ditch nor the bridge"[2] and suggested that "one may doubt the value of [Kant's last] work . . . without previous inspection if one considers both the frail state in which Kant was at the time, and the completion to which he himself had brought the philosophy which he had founded."[3] Yet we were deprived of this easy solution to our problem once the *Opus postumum* became available in the Academy edition in 1936 and 1938. The fascicles from the time in question do not bear the marks of senility. And, of course, neither do Kant's other productions from the same period. In the same year, 1798, Kant published his *Anthropology* and the *Conflict of the Faculties;* the *Metaphysics of Morals* had come out in the previous year. His correspondence from the same period likewise warrants no assumption of senility.

Although the suggestion of mental deterioration is no longer made, the general helplessness of the interpreter faced with Kant's remarks has remained. Allegations of senility have by and large given way to the charge that Kant misunderstood, or misdescribed, his own situation. Erich Adickes, a foremost Kant scholar and author of the first extensive study of the *Opus postumum,* contended that the goal Kant was aiming at in his last work was "a mere fata morgana," the alleged gap merely invented, and Kant's "time and labor" consequently "wasted."[4] Even the editor of the *Opus postumum* in the Academy edition of Kant's works, Gerhard Lehmann, felt compelled to write: "The 'gap' Kant talks about is not really a gap; the task he sets for himself is formally the same as the one set in the *Metaphysical Foundations of Natural Science*—namely, the application of the metaphysics of nature to physics."[5] On one point, however, Kant's commentators have always agreed: that "gap" and "transition" are but two sides of the same problem, and that the "Transition" was conceived by Kant to fill the alleged gap he had detected in his system.

I intend to question this widespread dogma of Kant scholarship.[6] Admittedly, Kant's own words seem to support the prevailing interpretation. To quote again from his letter to Garve: "The project on which I am now working concerns the 'Transition from the metaphysical foundations of natural science to physics.' It must be completed, or else a gap will remain in the critical philosophy." And on Leaf 5 of the fourth fascicle, Kant notes: "There is a gap to be filled between the metaphysical foundations of natural science and physics; its filling is called a transition from the one to the other" (21:482, Op. 43). These remarks seem to suggest not only a close proximity but also an interdependence of the discovered gap and the projected Transition.

Nevertheless, I believe this identification to be mistaken. My main reason for saying this is that Kant had been working on the Transition for several years before the alleged "gap" was mentioned for the first time. And it seems that Kant had been thinking about this project for even longer. In fact, the idea for such a work seems to go back at least to the year 1790. In June 1795, Kiesewetter had already reminded Kant that "for some years now" he had promised to present the public "with a few sheets that are to contain the transition from your *Metaphysical Foundations of Natural Science* to physics itself" (12:23). It is more than likely that Kant gave this promise of "some years" before when Kiesewetter had visited him in the fall of 1790. During the few weeks he stayed in Königsberg,[7] Kiesewetter frequently met with Kant to discuss difficult problems of the critical philosophy. In this context they also discussed, and did so extensively, Kant's *Metaphysical Foundations.* This is clear from the remainder of Kiesewetter's letter, where he says concerning this work: "I still recall with great gratitude that I owe its complete comprehension to your oral instruction." The main evidence comes, however, from a Preface and Introduction Kiesewetter wrote for a new edition of Kant's *Metaphysical Foundations,* which he intended to publish with his own annotations (but which did not materialize). Kiesewetter writes: "Several of the annotations which I have appended to the Kantian text were written down during my stay in Königsberg, and were read and approved by him. Others he himself dictated to me, for even then I had the plan (which he applauded) to publish explanatory notes to the said work."[8]

In this context, Kant must have expressed his own intention to write a "Transition" from the *Metaphysical Foundations of Natural Science* to physics. We can rule out the possibility that he later informed Kiesewetter of his plan in a letter, for soon after Kiesewetter's return to Berlin, Kant broke off all relations with him and did not write again until December 1793.[9] There is no mention of a "Transition" in this letter of Kant's, and a later communication that might have been lost would not fit Kiesewetter's expression "for some years now." The tone of Kiesewetter's letter also rules out the possibility that he had heard of Kant's project from a third person. I thus conclude that Kant must already have had a plan to write a Transition in 1790, when Kiesewetter visited him in Königsberg.

For reasons mentioned in Chapter 1, however, Kant's work on this project did not assume any systematic form until 1796. Even then, it is not for another two years (and more than 130 pages in the Academy edition) that the "gap" is mentioned for the first time. It is mentioned first in the loose leaves of the fourth fascicle that were written in 1798 (6, 3/4, 5, and 7), shortly before the letters to Garve and Kiesewetter. Fortunately, the dating here is incontestable. Two of the leaves (3/4 and 5) contain notes for the intended letter to Garve; his name is mentioned twice. There is also an allusion to Garve's *Übersicht der vornehmsten Prinzipien der Sittenlehre, von dem Zeitalter des Aristoteles an bis auf unsere Zeit,* which was dedicated to Kant and published in September of the same year (see 13:486f.). Kant received his complementary copy with Garve's accompanying letter on September 19, and his own reply is from September 21, so leaves 3/4 and 5 must have been written at least in part on these days. In these leaves mention of "a gap" is made for the first time—eight years after the expressed intention to write a science of transition! In view of this time lag, it seems utterly implausible that the Transition should be Kant's attempt to fill the "gap in the critical philosophy" that so worried him in 1798. It would seem much more likely that in that year Kant had reason to reflect anew on his critical system in such a way that it brought to his attention "a gap" that had previously escaped him. (I shall return to this point.) If we assume that the gap could only be bridged by the Transition on which Kant was working at the time, their juxtaposition in the letters to Garve and Kiesewetter could also be justified and intelligible. Presumably at this time Kant could only see *that,* but not yet *how,* the Transition must achieve this goal—hence the pain "like that of Tantalus." Or so I shall argue.

I begin by looking at the work from which the Transition is supposed to take its departure, the *Metaphysical Foundations of Natural Science.* Why did Kant write this book in 1785–86? What is its place in the Kantian oeuvre?

It is a commonplace that Kant thought of his transcendental work as preparatory, as a groundwork for a future metaphysics that deserved the name of a science. The task of the *Critique of Pure Reason* is accordingly to examine the origin, limit, and extent of possible a priori cognition. In the Architectonic chapter, Kant lays out in schematic form the plan for such future metaphysics in accordance with the critical standards: "Metaphysics is divided into that of the *speculative* and that of the *practical* employment of pure reason, and is therefore either *metaphysics of nature* or *metaphysics of morals* . . . [Metaphysics of nature] consists of four main parts: (1) ontology; (2) rational physiology; (3) rational cosmology; (4) rational theology. The second part, namely, the doctrine of nature as developed by pure reason, contains two divisions, *physica rationalis* and *psychologia rationalis*" (A841–847).

The *Critique of Pure Reason* had prepared the ground for such a metaphysical system. In its Preface, Kant thus announced: "Such a system of pure (speculative) reason I hope myself to produce under the title Metaphysics of Nature" (Axxi). Oddly enough, he never produced such a work. Whereas the often announced *Metaphysics of Morals* eventually appeared in 1797, there is no work entitled *Metaphysics of Nature.* In 1786, five years after the first *Critique,* Kant published a text with a similar title, the *Metaphysical Foundations of Natural Science.* That this work is not identical with the envisaged metaphysics of nature is clear from the Preface to the second edition of the *Critique,* written one year after the *Metaphysical Foundations,* where Kant again expresses his hope of providing "a metaphysics of nature and morals which will confirm the truth of my Critique in the two fields, of speculative and of practical reason" (Bxliii). In other words, these works had not yet been written. What, then, is the role of the *Metaphysical Foundations* in Kant's system?

If we go by the first edition of the *Critique,* the answer seems easy: it is a part of the metaphysical system. It is the first subdivision of rational physiology, namely, *physica rationalis.* But if we turn to the *Metaphysical Foundations* itself, we notice that it is not—or, I should say, it is no longer—a part of the metaphysical system. For in its Preface Kant declares:

> Metaphysics has engaged so many heads up till now and will continue to engage them not in order to extend natural knowledge (which comes about much more easily and certainly by observation, experiment, and the application of mathematics to external phenomena), but in order to attain to a

knowledge of what lies entirely beyond all boundaries of experience, namely God, freedom, and im-
mortality. If these things are so, then one gains
when he frees general metaphysics from a shoot
springing indeed from its own roots but only hin-
dering its regular growth, and plants this shoot
apart. (4:477)

Rational physics, the metaphysical doctrine of body, is thus
to become a "separate system," a shoot planted apart to prevent any hindrance of the growth of general metaphysics,
whose real interest concerns that which lies beyond all
boundaries of experience. This separation, Kant insists, does
not entail ignoring the origination of the shoot from its roots,
nor does it affect the completeness of the system of general
metaphysics; rather, it "facilitates the uniform progress" of
the latter system.

On closer inspection, however, this explanation raises
more questions than it answers. Is it really plausible that
Kant should suddenly have remembered that metaphysics
aims at the supersensible, whereas the metaphysical doctrine
of body does not? And even if this were so, why did he work
out this "separate system" first, and not, as promised, the
"Metaphysics of Nature"? For it is very noteworthy that
Kant had nowhere previously expressed his intentions to
write *Metaphysical Foundations of Natural Science*—except
in his famous letter to Lambert of December 31, 1765. That
fell, however, into Kant's so-called empiricist phase; *Anfangs-
gründe* then had quite a different function. Since the divisions
of metaphysics were still seen as stemming from the nature of
what exists rather than from "the essential nature of the
thinking faculty itself" (4:472), metaphysical "foundations"
of natural and practical philosophy had to *precede* the philosophical analysis and, by providing cases *in concreto*, vouch-
safe the correctness of its methodological procedure.[10] This

became superfluous precisely with Kant's critical turn.[11] The *Metaphysical Foundations* of 1786 arrived unannounced and unexpectedly—out of the blue, so to speak. Why?

There is only one place I know of where Kant explicitly comments on the origin of this work, namely, in a letter of September 13, 1785, to Christian Gottfried Schütz, written shortly after the completion of its main text. Kant here gives two reasons why the new work had to precede the often promised metaphysics of nature. The first is the same as the one we just encountered, namely, that metaphysics must be pure and homogeneous and hence must not contain any empirical elements.[12] Yet, obviously, this fails to explain why the *Metaphysical Foundations* had to *precede* metaphysics. More interesting, therefore, is the second reason. Kant writes: "Before I can compose the Metaphysics of Nature, which I have promised to do, I had to write something that is in fact a mere application of it but that presupposes an *empirical* concept. I refer to the metaphysical foundations of the doctrine of body . . . I wanted to have some instances *in concreto* available to which I could refer in order to make my discourse comprehensible" (10:406).

This sudden need for instances *in concreto* is also emphasized in the Preface to the *Metaphysical Foundations* itself. As Kant puts it there: "A separate metaphysics of corporeal nature does excellent and *indispensable* service to general metaphysics, inasmuch as the former provides instances (cases *in concreto*) in which to realize the concepts and propositions of the latter (properly, transcendental philosophy), i.e., to give to a mere form of thought sense and meaning" (4:478; first italics mine).

This sounds as if transcendental philosophy, without the aid of a separate metaphysics of corporeal nature, must be void of "sense and meaning." Yet had not the *Critique* insisted that the pure concepts and principles of transcendental philosophy gain their meaning from their relation to possible experience? Was not a chief purpose of the *Critique* the demonstration that the categories must be limited in their application to appearances, and that once this condition is removed, "all meaning, that is, relation to the object, falls away" (A 241)? At the same time, Kant singled out as "the peculiarity" of transcendental philosophy the fact that besides the rule which is given in the pure concept of the understanding, it can "also specify a priori the instance to which the rule is to be applied" (A135). And, as he insisted, transcendental philosophy must be able to do this, for the objective validity of its concepts could never be demonstrated a posteriori: "It must formulate by means of universal but sufficient marks the conditions under which objects can be given in harmony with these concepts. Otherwise the concepts would be void of all content, and therefore be mere logical forms, not pure concepts of the understanding" (A136). This demonstration of the objective validity of the categories is undertaken in the Schematism chapter. The schemata "first realize the categories." They are "the true and sole conditions" under which categories obtain relation to an object. Properly speaking, Kant explains, the schema is nothing but "the sensible concept of an object in agreement with the category" (A146).

Although Kant's insistence on the necessary restriction of all categories to, and realization in, possible intuition is a theme that runs through his entire critical work, a subtle shift in his position takes place between the first and second editions of the *Critique*. As has often been noted, the following passage from the Phenomena and Noumena chapter occurs only in the first edition: "There is something strange and even absurd in the assertion that there should be a concept which possesses a meaning and yet is not capable of any explanation. But the categories have this peculiar feature, that only in virtue of the general condition of sensibility can they possess a determinate meaning and relation to any object . . .

Consequently, the categories require, in addition to the pure concept of understanding, determinations of their application to sensibility in general (schemata)" (A244–245).

Instead of this omitted passage, Kant adds in the second edition a General Note to the System of the Principles. It opens by echoing the omitted remark just quoted from A, pointing out the "very noteworthy fact" that in order to exhibit the objective reality of a category one must always have an intuition. This time, however, Kant adds: "But it is an even more noteworthy fact, that in order to understand the possibility of things in conformity with the categories and so to demonstrate the *objective reality* of the latter, we need, not merely intuitions, but intuitions that are in all cases *outer intuitions*" (B288–291).

Undoubtedly this shift of emphasis, from intuition as such to outer intuition, is directly attributable to the intervening publication of the *Metaphysical Foundations.* For there the indispensability of outer intuitions is stressed for the first time, and almost with the exact same words: "It is indeed very remarkable (but cannot here be thoroughly entered into) that general metaphysics in all cases where it requires instances (intuitions) in order to provide meaning for its pure concepts of the understanding must always take such instances from the general doctrine of body, i.e., from the form and principles of external intuition, and if these instances are not at hand in their entirety, it gropes, uncertain and trembling, among mere meaningless concepts" (4:478).

Here we get a first glimpse of the real importance of the *Metaphysical Foundations,* and of its relation to the first *Critique.* For precisely by laying out the principles of *external* intuition *in their entirety* does it prevent the *Critique* from groping "uncertain and trembling, among mere meaningless concepts." Is it mere coincidence when, after the task is completed, Kant returns in the Preface to the second edition of the *Critique* to this metaphor of groping among concepts?

Hardly. By this time, however, he is in a position to employ it differently, namely, to denounce all previous metaphysics whose procedure, owing to its lack of a relation to possible intuition, had been "a merely random groping, and what is worst of all, a groping among mere concepts" (Bxv).

Thus it becomes clear why it was instrumental for Kant to delay the work on the projected system of metaphysics and to work out first a "separate metaphysics of corporeal nature": it is nothing less than the belated demonstration of the real applicability and objective validity of the pure categories and principles of the understanding. The Schematism chapter, it is true, had also promised to specify the conditions under which an object may be given *"in concreto"* (A138) in accordance with the categories. Moreover, it had promised to formulate these conditions by means of "universal but sufficient marks," since otherwise the categories would be "void of all content, and therefore mere logical forms, not pure concepts of the understanding" (A136).

It now turns out, however, that this latter promise had not been completely redeemed. Since the Schematism chapter dealt exclusively with time determinations and inner sense,[13] it did not specify the "sufficient" conditions of the application of the categories; it required supplementation by a work that laid out the forms and principles of *outer* intuition in their entirety, and thus related the categories to possible objects of outer intuition.[14] In this manner alone was it possible to secure completely their objective validity and to relieve them from the potential charge of being empty concepts. Thus we may well take Kant at his word when, in the Preface to the *Metaphysical Foundations,* he insists that this separate metaphysics of corporeal nature does an "indispensible" service to general metaphysics by providing "instances (cases *in concreto*) in which to realize the propositions of . . . transcendental philosophy," thus giving "to a mere form of thought sense and meaning" (4:478).[15]

It is not very difficult to see what must have led to the revision of Kant's position. In 1782, a first, eagerly awaited review of the *Critique* came to Kant's notice. It characterized his position as a "system of higher idealism" that transforms "the world and us into representations," and, moreover, expressly linked it with the idealism of Berkeley, whose *Dialogues* had also appeared (in German translation) in the previous year, attracting considerable attention.[16]

One can, I think, scarcely overestimate the importance of this review for the further development of Kant's position. His immediate reaction is well known. In three notes (§13) and an Appendix to the *Prolegomena,* Kant tried to defend himself against the "unpardonable and almost intentional misconception" of linking his critical position to the "phantasms" that he considered Berkeley's "mystical and visionary idealism" to be. Unlike himself, Kant insists, Berkeley cannot distinguish truth from illusion and hence can have "no criteria of truth," because he regards space as a merely empirical representation, not as a priori in origin (4:290, 293, 375). The argument is not convincing as it stands; yet its main point is further developed and eventually finds a more forceful expression in the Refutation of Idealism and in the General Note on the System of the Principles in the second edition of the *Critique:* all experience, as involving change, requires something permanent in perception in relation to which the alterations can be determined. Yet what allows us to represent something as abiding during change is the *simultaneity* of its manifold. And we can represent a manifold as simultaneous only because we have the *original* representation of space.

This argument, quite clearly, has implications beyond the narrow confines of idealism, and Kant was in no doubt about them: "These remarks are of great importance, not only in confirmation of our previous refutation of idealism, but even more, when we come to treat of *self-knowledge* by mere inner consciousness, that is, by determination of our nature without the aid of *outer empirical intuitions*—as showing us the limits of the possibility of this kind of knowledge" (B293f.; second italics mine).

Thus we have reached an answer to the question posed above: the *Metaphysical Foundations* was written in order to supplement the Schematism and to complete the proof of the objective validity of the categories. As such, it could no longer be a part of the metaphysical system, of the metaphysics of nature, but had to precede it.

What does a proof of the objective validity of the categories for outer objects look like? In general, Kant maintains, for a concept or representation to have objective validity, its corresponding object must be capable of being given. That the concept is noncontradictory shows only the *logical* possibility of its object, not that anything corresponds to it: "I can *think* whatever I please, provided only that I do not contradict myself" (Bxxvii). To prove the objective validity of a concept is thus to demonstrate the 'real' possibility of its object. In empirical knowledge, the real possibility of an object is proven by its actuality. In the case of a priori knowledge, by contrast, I must show that the intuition corresponding to the concept can be given a priori, or that the concept can be constructed.

In other words, to cognize a priori the objective validity of the categories for "a something that is to be an object of the external senses," this concept, or the concept of matter in general (4:476), must be constructed. To this end the *Metaphysical Foundations* was written: "Therefore, the concept of matter had to be carried out through all the four functions of the concepts of the understanding . . . Under the four classes of quantity, quality, relation, and finally modality, all determinations of the universal concept of a matter in general . . . must be capable of being brought" (4:474–476). By providing the principles for the construction of "matter" in this way, Kant's metaphysics of nature permits one "to realize the concepts and propositions of [transcendental philosophy], i.e., to give to a mere form of thought sense and meaning" (4:478).

To do so, however, it must lay at its basis the analysis of an empirical concept. Whereas the first *Critique* had described the laws that make possible the concept of nature in general, taking "no notice of objects that may be given" (A845), its metaphysical counterpart treats of a particular nature, particularized by the form of outer sense in which objects may be given, and in which the transcendental principles are to be applied and realized. Yet that outer sense is not empty cannot be known a priori: existence cannot be constructed.[17]

The task of a construction of the concept 'matter' thus really has two sides to it. The *Metaphysical Foundations* must first take the empirical concept of matter in general and determine what a priori cognitions are possible with regard to it. That is, it must analyze this concept and discern the fundamental properties that belong to the possibility of matter in general (4:472). It must then, second, demonstrate how the concept 'matter' can be constructed from the elements thus gained. It must show, in other words, how to exhibit a priori the intuition that corresponds to the concept. Let us look more closely, then, at Kant's text from this point of view.

In the Dynamics chapter we are shown, first, that two fundamental forces, attraction and repulsion, are required for the filling of a space to a determinate degree, for what distinguishes matter from the space it occupies is the fact that it resists all forces that try to enter into the same space.[18] This it cannot do by its mere existence, Kant argues, but only by a special moving force which he calls "driving" (*treibende*) or "repulsive" force. To fill a space to a determinate degree, however, a second force is required that opposes the first and limits its expansion, that is, a "drawing" *(ziehende)* or "attractive" force. Neither force can in principle suffice on its own: without attraction, matter would by its repulsive force disperse itself to infinity, leaving space empty; without repulsion, matter would by its attractive force coalesce into a single point, again leaving space empty. Therefore, it is only by the interaction of both fundamental forces that matter of a determinate quantity is possible. And more than two fundamental forces of matter, Kant held, "cannot be thought" (4:498, 511).

Second, to construct the concept of matter from these two forces, we need a law that determines the approach or withdrawal of the parts of matter: "a law of the relation both of original attraction and of original repulsion at various distances of matter and of its parts from one another" (4:517). To determine the precise nature of this law, Kant is eager to emphasize, is a mathematical problem, not a metaphysical one. For it depends entirely on the difference of direction of these two forces, and on the size of the space into which each of them diffuses itself at various distances. Potential problems with the construction of the concept of matter in this way thus fall outside the responsibility of metaphysics. Its task is merely to guarantee "the correctness of the elements of the construction that are granted our rational cognition" (4:517).

But why should there be any problems? Kant had stated the respective laws for both the attractive and repulsive forces as early as 1756 in his *Monadologia physica*. There he argued that since the repulsive force acts outward from a central point of the space occupied by the material element, its intensity will diminish in inverse proportion to the space through which it exerts itself, for such a force could not be found to be efficacious in a determinate sphere unless it filled by its action the entire space comprehended by the given diameter. Hence, repulsion will be in inverse ratio of the cubes of the distances from the center. Attraction acts in the opposite direction; hence it will be the spherical surface toward which the attraction is exercised at a given distance. It can be represented in terms of straight lines that emanate from the surface toward the central point. Since the multitude of the spherical points is determined, so is the magnitude of the attraction: it will decrease in the inverse ratio of the spherical surfaces, that is, with the inverse square of the distances. And Kant here refers explicitly to the discussion of gravitational attraction by the Newtonian John Keill to illustrate the latter law (see 2:484).

The same laws are also assigned to attraction and repulsion in the *Metaphysical Foundations*. Thus Kant writes: "The original attraction of matter would act in inverse proportion to the square of the distance at all distances and the original repulsion in inverse proportion to the cube of the infinitely small distances. By such an action and reaction of both fundamental forces, matter would be possible by a determinate degree of the filling of its space" (4:521). The differences in the ratio of their diminishing intensity will lead to points of equilibrium that determine the degree to which the space is filled with matter.

Nevertheless, Kant admits a difficulty with this explanation that he addresses in the subsequent note. This difficulty consists in the fact that, on the one hand, his theory of matter is now (unlike in 1756)[19] based on the assumption that matter is a continuum and is thus infinitely divisible into parts that are themselves matter (according to Proposition 4). Hence no actual distances must be assumed between them. On the other hand, we visualize the repulsion between two parts of matter in terms of infinitely small distances, because every part of a space filled by matter must of itself be movable.

This problem, which Kant also addresses in the proof and notes to Proposition 4, is given the following solution. Since there is no difference between an infinitely small intermediate space and actual contact, the problem arises only from the conflict between the principle of construction, on the one hand, and our attempt to visualize the expansion of matter, on the other: "When it is said, then, that the repulsive force of the directly mutually driving parts of matter stand in inverse proportion to the cube of their distances, this means only that they stand in inverse proportion to the corporeal space which one thinks of between parts that nevertheless immediately touch each other, and whose distance must for this reason be termed infinitely small in order that such distance may be distinguished from all actual distance" (4:522).

In the *Metaphysical Foundations* Kant leaves it at this, and for good reasons. The actual exposition of the law of an original repulsion is not essential to his theory; it suffices to have provided the elements for a construction of the concept of matter: "disputes and doubts" (4:523) which might befall this exposition of the law of repulsion, he insists, must not be mixed up with the theory itself. A different law for the repulsive force would not falsify the claim that it is in principle possible to construct the concept of matter from the two fundamental forces of attraction and repulsion and their respective laws. Yet possible it must be, at least in principle, if the *Metaphysical Foundations* is to achieve its intended goal. Thus it is important not to confuse the "difficulty" mentioned here[20] with the "impossibility" of a construction Kant speaks of later, in the General Observation to Dynamics (see 4:525). For there Kant speaks of the *specific variety* of matter that cannot be constructed within a dynamical theory of matter, and whose moments he therefore merely lists, "as I hope, completely"—moments such as fluidity, rigidity, brittleness, elasticity, and so on. These remarks are preceded by an explicit warning that one must guard against going beyond what makes possible the universal concept of matter in general, and not try to construct the particular and specific varieties of matter. For once the "material" *(Stoff)* that the atomist regards as "completely homogeneous" is "transformed into fundamental forces," these moments can no longer be constructed. They cannot be constructed because the laws governing these *specific* forces cannot be determined a priori: all we can know is that they must belong to, or be varieties of, "the repulsive forces in general and the attractive forces in general" (4:524).[21]

As we saw in the preceding chapter, however, Kant soon came to realize that his explanation of the possibility of an object of outer sense is affected by a problem much more fundamental than the precise nature of the law for repulsion; moreover, it is a problem concerning attraction. By 1792 he had concluded that his construction of the differences of density in matter was circular, and that gravitational attraction could not figure as the second fundamental force in the construction of 'matter'. The question he had to address, therefore, was "whether apart from universal attraction there be another one which acts originally, according to different laws?" (21:430). It soon became clear to him that, instead of attraction at a distance, attraction in contact, that is, cohesion, must be assumed to counterbalance the original force of repulsion. Consequently, the law governing cohesion must replace the law of gravitational attraction in the construction of the dynamical concept of matter.

The further development of Kant's thinking on this topic is not easy to discern in the preserved text of the *Opus postumum*. As his work on the Transition progresses, questions of detail in the theory of matter get interspersed with attempts at a systematic classification of the moving forces of matter, or the determination of matter's fundamental properties in accordance with the categories. A large number of different problems occupy Kant at the same time and leave their sometimes confusing traces in the early drafts of the *Opus postumum*. Rarely is a single problem pursued continuously for more than a few paragraphs. Nevertheless, one can perhaps distinguish roughly four stages or steps in the further development of Kant's thinking, insofar as it relates to the construction of matter.

1. On the early leaves of this work, we find Kant explicitly addressing the question: Is cohesion a form of original attraction? Since cohesion is a surface force, it cannot be characterized by the inverse-square law as is gravitational attraction. But is it a genuine attraction at all? In his attempts to answer this question, Kant first considers Galileo's suggestion[22] to determine the degree of cohesion by measuring the weight at which a uniform prism or cylinder breaks at a certain length as the result of its own weight (21:417, Op. 4). He soon reaches the result that "the cohesion of types of matter . . . cannot rest on their inner force of attraction" (21:406, Op. 18). Consequently, cohesion is possible only through an external force. Yet it cannot stem from pressure, which would not permit alterations of the figures of fluids, but only from the "living force" of impact (see 21:454, 389, Op. 5, 14, and so on). Thus Kant concludes that cohesion must be the result of the *pulsations* of the ether (see 21:333.14–20 and 21:378, Op. 12). As such, he writes, cohesion is "essentially different from the attraction of gravitation. If it were a genuine [*eigenthümliche*] force of attraction (not resulting from impact) it would be subject to the law of the inverse square of the distance" (21:468.11–14). Since it is not, to what law is cohesion subject?

2. The next drafts ("A"–"C," "α"–"ε") deal primarily with the classification of the moving forces of matter according to the table of categories while also developing further the theory of the formation of bodies from the original dissolution of all materials in the universally distributed ether or caloric. At the same time, Kant tries to gain further clarity about cohesion and the different types of attraction. The problem is discussed in the form of various specific examples of apparent attraction, and of their dependence on ether-oscillations: "the

apparent attraction and repulsion in capillary tubes" (21:308, Op. 24), in the formation of droplets (21:521, Op. 34), and others.

3. As a third step we might describe the general reassessment of the various elements of his theory of matter as it has developed so far. In a way, reflections and reevaluations of this kind accompany Kant's work on the Transition throughout, but they become more intensified at times when a position is about to undergo revisions. Such meta-reflections are recorded primarily in the margins of his sheets, and also on the wrappers of his fascicles. These function as notebooks for Kant, whereas the main parts of the sheets are reserved for his drafts of a continuous text. Of interest in the present case is the wrapper of the fourth fascicle, since it also holds the loose leaves 6, 3/4, 5, and 7 that we encountered in connection with Garve, and on which the "gap" in the critical philosophy is mentioned for the first time. On this wrapper we notice several brief returns to questions of the *Metaphysical Foundations*. On its second page, for example, we find again a polemic against the mathematical or atomistic explanation of the differences of density familiar from the text of 1786, followed by a renewed definition of matter: "Matter can be defined in two different ways (in contrast with form), namely, [in terms of] its expansion of space and [in terms of] its motion in time.—Matter is what fills space, or also is the movable in space" (21:340.25–28). With regard to the ether on which cohesion and hence the formation of bodies is said to depend, Kant notes: "An imponderable matter of which one thinks that it penetrates all bodies (heat) is originally elastic and not coercible . . . and acts in cubic ratio of its expansion" (21:348.9–13). And about the impacts this elastic yet imponderable matter exerts on the bodies it penetrates, Kant records: "The effect of bodily impact does not, as it were, arouse the reaction, nor does the motion flow, entirely or partly, into the other body through

transfusion *(accidentia migrant e substantiis in substantiis);* rather, the motion of impact is possible only through antagonism" (21:351.20–24).

4. What is left now is to bring these scattered remarks to bear on the problem at hand. Kant begins Leaf 6 of the fourth fascicle with renewed statements of why a transition from the metaphysical foundations of natural science to physics is needed: "These two territories (metaphysics of nature and physics) do not immediately come into contact . . . Rather, there exists a gulf between the two, over which philosophy must build a bridge in order to reach the opposite bank." (21:475, Op. 39) Clearly, this "gulf" that the Transition must bridge, as separating the metaphysical from the empirical study of natural objects, cannot yet be the gap in the *critical* philosophy that Kant laments in his letters to Garve and Kiesewetter. And also the opening passages of the second page of this leaf do not go beyond what is altogether familiar by now. After another classification of the moving forces in terms of attraction, repulsion, impact, and penetration, however, Kant continues: "Physics is the doctrine of the laws of the moving forces of matter. Since the latter, like everything belonging to the existence of things, must be known by experience [*breaks off*] How does matter produce a body?" (21:476, Op. 40–41).

This passage is interesting for several reasons. Why does Kant break off the second sentence? For it seems clear, at least from the *Metaphysical Foundations,* how it would have to be continued. In 1786 Kant had written: "Natural science properly so called presupposes metaphysics of nature; for laws, i.e., principles of the necessity of what belongs to the existence of a thing, are occupied with a concept that does not admit of construction, because existence cannot be presented in any a priori intuition . . . Therefore, in order to cognize the possibility of determinate natural things, and hence to cognize them a priori, there is further required that the intuition corresponding to the concept be given a priori, i.e., that the concept be constructed" (4:469–470).

Thus it is easy to imagine how Kant's passage from Leaf 6 would have to be completed: Physics is the doctrine of the laws of the moving forces of matter. Since the latter, like everything belonging to the existence of things, must be known by experience, *physics presupposes metaphysical foundations in which the possibility of an outer object is cognized a priori, that is, this concept is constructed.* But Kant does not complete the sentence; instead he asks: How does matter produce a body?

So let us try to answer this question, too. A material body is produced originally from the interplay of two opposing forces: attraction and repulsion. As we know by now, the attraction that counterbalances the original force of repulsion must be cohesion. Can the concept of matter be constructed from these forces? For this to be possible, Kant had explained in the *Metaphysical Foundations,* we need in addition to the two fundamental forces "a law of the relation both of original attraction and original repulsion at various distances of matter and of its parts from one another." But now, it seems, we run into a difficulty.

The force of cohesion is not a universal and penetrative force like gravitation, but a superficial force, or surface force, acting only in contact. In this respect, then, it is like repulsion. But it must not obey the same law that repulsion does, for this would make impossible the explanation of the formation of bodies given in the *Metaphysical Foundations.* Only the interplay of two forces of *different* measure can explain how matter sets limits to itself and forms a body: because repulsion increases in greater measure upon approach of the parts of a matter than attraction does, there will be an equilibrium of the forces marking the "limit of approach" (4:521)—the surface of the body—beyond which no greater approach is possible for the given attraction. If both forces decrease in the same proportion to the distances, no account can be given in the dynamical theory of matter of how to exhibit a priori in intuition the differences in volume and density. In other words, the concept of "a something that is to be an object of the external senses" would no longer be constructible.

But is this result inevitable? It may be objected that it does not follow, at least not obviously so, that because cohesion is a surface force, it must decrease in inverse proportion to the cube of its distances. Why should all surface forces obey this law? In the *Metaphysical Foundations*, the derivation of the inverse-cube law is explicitly tied to repulsion, as elasticity of parts of matter in proportion to the spaces into which they are compressed (see 4:505). It is not obvious that the same argument could be applied to cohesion. What rules out the possibility that cohesion is a surface force that decreases in inverse proportion to the square of its distances?

Here we must remember that Kant reached a twofold result with regard to the force of cohesion. First, unlike gravitational attraction, it is not a penetrative force but a contact force. And second, it is not a genuine form of attraction at all but itself the effect of repulsion—the result of the impact of the unceasing ether-oscillations. The cohering parts of a body are in effect pushed together (see, e.g., 21:383.27–31). Hence the forces of both repulsion and cohesion must be represented as increasing or decreasing in the same proportion to the distances of the parts of matter on which they act. Although this model allows Kant to avoid the circularity in his theory of matter of 1786 discussed earlier, one of its problematic results is that the formation of an object of outer sense from these forces can no longer be constructed in pure intuition.

Kant's revised theory of matter is thus afflicted with a serious problem. The same characterization now applies to it that, in the *Metaphysical Foundations*, Kant had used with regard to chemistry:

> So long, then, as there is for the chemical actions of
> matter on one another no concept which admits of
> being constructed, i.e., no law of the approach or
> withdrawal of the parts of matters can be stated ac-
> cording to which (as, say, in proportion to their
> densities and suchlike) their motions together with
> the consequences of these can be intuited and pre-
> sented a priori in space (a demand that will hardly
> ever be fulfilled), chemistry can become nothing
> more than a systematic art or experimental doc-
> trine, but never science proper. (4:470f.)

The full implications of Kant's reflections in the loose leaves
of the fourth fascicle become clear, however, only if we recall
the role the *Metaphysical Foundations* was to play within
Kant's system. Earlier I argued that the function of the *Metaphysical Foundations* was not merely to provide a metaphysical basis for physics, and thus to render comprehensible the
apodictic certainty in the cognition of its laws, but also, and
more important, to complete the proof of the objective validity of the pure categories and principles of the understanding.
This work was required to perform the "indispensible service" of providing instances *in concreto* in which to realize
these principles, and hence "to give to a mere form of
thought sense and meaning."

But if the object of the outer sense in general can no longer
be constructed, transcendental philosophy itself is again in
need of the "indispensible service" the *Metaphysical Foundations* promised to provide, namely, to ascertain its objective
validity and real applicability. This indispensible service—if it
is still possible after all—must hence employ other means
than mathematical construction. But which ones? What
could those be? Suddenly, a real "gap" opens up—a gap,
moreover, in the *critical* system.[23]

If this interpretation is correct, "gap" and "transition" signify different, and independent, problems in Kant. Work on the projected Transition was long under way when Kant realized that the revisions and modifications that he had to undertake in his dynamical theory of matter had opened up a gap in his critical system that was severe enough to remind him of the pain of Tantalus. Seventeen years after the publication of the *Critique of Pure Reason,* the question of the objective validity of its concepts and principles still awaited a satisfactory demonstration.

If this interpretation is correct, one would expect to find the Transition project redescribed, or characterized differently, in the sheets that succeed Kant's discovery of the gap in his system. This is indeed the case. How would one best characterize a doctrine whose task it was to demonstrate the objective validity and real applicability of a priori concepts? As a schematism of these concepts. And thus the project is suddenly characterized. The Transition, Kant now says, is "a schematism of the concepts of metaphysics" (21:169.21). Its absence, he adds, would "commit the propositions of philosophy to the play of opinions and hypotheses" (21: 177.25–26)—to a mere random groping among concepts, one is tempted to add in the words of the earlier Kant.

There is yet another redescription of the Transition project that is worth noting. It occurs in the letter to Kiesewetter cited at the beginning of this chapter. Kiesewetter was of course well acquainted with the idea of a Transition. After all, it was he who had reminded Kant of this project in 1795. Would Kant explain to him, when reporting of his work on it, what the Transition was, as he did to the uninitiated Garve? Hardly. And if we read carefully, we notice that here Kant does not so much say what the Transition consists in as what he now intends *to do* with it. He writes: "I want to make [*ausarbeiten*] the Transition from the metaphysical foundations of natural science to physics *into a special part* of the natural philosophy [*als einen eigenen Teil der philosophia naturalis*]" (12:258, cf., e.g., 21:622.6–14). Yet only a few months earlier—according to Adickes, between July 1797 and July 1798—Kant had still maintained that the Transition was "not a particular part ... of ... *philosophia naturalis*" (21:527, Op. 38). I take this to mean that the Transition, which had occupied Kant for almost a decade, is now assigned a new role or function in his system. If the object of outer sense in general cannot be constructed, the Transition can no longer have merely the function of providing a "sketch of a system" for physics. Rather, in the absence of any conceivable alternative, it must henceforth also assume the task previously assigned to the *Metaphysical Foundations of Natural Science:* of ascertaining the objective validity and real applicability of the pure concepts of the understanding. Nothing but the Transition *could* take on this task, although it is not clear to Kant at all at this time how, in detail, this might be done. It took him quite some time and several attempts in other directions until he realized that only the exhibition of the subject's own bodily forces in the systematization of experience can play the role previously assigned to the construction of the concept 'matter'. In other words, only a *Selbstsetzungslehre* can fill the "gap" in the critical system. It is to this doctrine that we must turn next.[24]

CHAPTER FOUR

Ether Proof
and *Selbstsetzungslehre*

To engage in a serious study of Kant's *Opus postumum* is still
a solitary task. This seems especially true of the *Selbstsetzungslehre* of the last fascicles, that is, the doctrine that the
subject posits itself, or makes itself into an object of experience. Although clearly the culmination of Kant's last work—
if not, as I am inclined to think, of his entire critical
philosophy—this doctrine has received only the scantest attention. Erich Adickes, whose influential study predated the
publication of the *Opus postumum* in the Academy edition
by almost two decades and set the tone for much of what was
to come, failed to see in this doctrine any "real extension or
fortunate development of the Kantian system,"[1] and he was
"certain" that Kant's deliberate talk of "self-positing" was a
mere concession to Fichte and other "extreme" idealists, in-
dicative of Kant's desperate attempts to unify and consolidate
his disintegrating school. Distinguishing among six different
ways in which Kant allegedly used the term "self-positing" in
the *Opus postumum,* Adickes was convinced that these subtleties were Kant's misguided attempt to outclass Fichte and

all those "for whom excessive conceptual hair-splitting and a scholastic obsession with subtleties had become the mark of true philosophy."[2] No longer at the height of his powers, Kant had succumbed to what Adickes called the general "posito-mania" *(Setzkrankheit)* of the time.[3]

I find Adickes's conjecture implausible. Kant speaks of self-positing at a time when he was still working on the critical texts—a time, that is, before Fichte had even turned to philosophy. For his discussions with Kiesewetter sometime between 1788 and 1790, Kant writes that "I posit my own existence" in a world "for the sake of empirical consciousness and its possibility," because empirical knowledge of myself as a being determined in time can only be knowledge of "myself as a being that exists in a world" (18:615). He adds: "First we are an object of outer sense for ourselves, for otherwise we would not perceive our place in the world and could not intuit ourselves in relation to other things" (18:619).[4]

Clearly, Kant is drawing an important consequence from his Refutation of Idealism in the first *Critique,* namely, that if, for the temporal determination of my own consciousness, there must exist things outside me, then I must also exist in space and occupy a position in space to which other things can be external. How this is to be thought of, however, especially since space is not something outside me but only the subjective form of outer intuition, remains unclear in this context.

There are, of course, similar passages in the first *Critique* itself. For instance: "The 'I think' expresses the act of determining my existence. Existence is already given thereby, but the mode in which I am to determine this existence, that is, how I am to posit in me the manifold belonging to it, is not thereby given" (B158a; cf. B67f.).

But how am I to posit in me the manifold belonging to my own existence, in such a way as to determine this existence? Kant's *Opus postumum* provides an answer to this question. In order to understand fully the *Selbstsetzungslehre* of this work, however, it will be important to bear in mind what preceded it, and how it draws on and incorporates elements from various earlier stages of Kant's philosophical career. This means elements from Kant's early onto-theology, from the Dialectic of the first *Critique,* and especially from the mature ether theory of the *Opus postumum,* which sets the stage for, and provides a key to, the doctrine of self-positing.

─◦─

Let us begin by clarifying what Kant means by "positing." In his 1763 essay *The One Possible Basis for a Demonstration of God's Existence,* Kant for the first time expresses his famous thesis that existence is not a real predicate or determination of a thing. In this context, he also explicates the term "positing": "The concept of position or positing is completely simple and identical with the concept of being in general" (2:73). Being, Kant explains, is expressed in two fundamentally different ways: either in the copula in a judgment 'x is p', where the predicate is posited in relation to the subject; or in an existential proposition 'x is (exists)'. Kant calls the former the relative position, in which a further predicate is posited in relation to the subject. In the latter, the subject itself, with all its predicates, is posited outside the concept or the judger. This Kant calls the absolute position, or existence.

> If I say: "God is an existent thing," it seems as though I am expressing the relation of a predicate to a subject. However, there is an inaccuracy in this expression. Correctly speaking, one should say: "Something existent is God," that is, "There is an existent thing to whom belong those predicates which, taken together, we signify by the expression 'God'." These predicates are posited relative to the

subject, but the thing itself, together with all its predicates, is posited absolutely. (2:74)

The proof Kant provides for the existence of such a being is an adaptation of an argument developed in the *Nova dilucidatio* of 1755. The earlier version, in the seventh proposition of that work, proceeds from the notion of 'the possibility of all things' and continues roughly as follows: to say that something is possible is to say that the concepts that are compared or related in a judgment do not contradict one another but are compatible. We may call this the formal condition of possibility. There is also a material condition. In all comparison, what is to be compared—the material—must be given beforehand. Where there is nothing to be compared, there can be no comparison and hence no possibility. For Kant, this means that nothing can be conceived as possible unless whatever is real in every possible notion exists—and, he adds, exists with absolute necessity, because in its absence nothing would be possible, and possibility itself would be abolished, which is impossible. Furthermore, Kant argues, all these realities *(omnimoda haec realitas),* which in a sense are the material for all possible notions, can exist necessarily only if they are united in a single infinite being. For if the realities were distributed among several existing things, any of them would have its existence limited by privations that belong to the thoroughgoing determination of any existing finite thing. But absolute necessity does not belong to such privations in the way it belongs to the realities in question; the degree to which the realities were limited by privations would thus be a matter of contingency; hence, realities limited in this manner would also exist contingently. To enjoy absolute necessity, the realities in question must exist without any limitations whatsoever: they must constitute a single, infinite being, an *omnitudo realitatis.* This being we may call God, who is thus the absolutely necessary principle of all possibility. He is also, Kant adds, the ontological ground of the unity of our experience, which is single and all-embracing. This unity would be "unthinkable," Kant maintains, unless all finite substances "are maintained, in mutual relations, by their common ground *(principio),* namely, the divine intellect" (1:414, 413).

The argument just sketched leaves undetermined how the realities, the material for all possible notions, are supposed to be given to the human mind. The explication of Proposition 10 of *Nova dilucidatio* makes clear, however, that Kant here endorses Leibniz's idea that to the soul there is always internally present, albeit only in a dark and obscure fashion, an infinite perception of the whole universe *(infinita, quae semper animae interne praesto est, quanquam oscura admodum totius universi perceptio),* which already contains within itself whatever realities must be in those thoughts that are afterward to be illuminated with greater light, when we deliberately focus attention on them. In this way, we constantly increase our knowledge, through ever new combinations, limitations, and determinations of what is present to our mind, although "the material of all representations derived from their connection with the universe remains the same" (1:408). Yet "that there is anything at all which can be thought, from which, through combination, limitation, and determination, there subsequently results the notion of any conceivable thing—this would be unintelligible unless whatever is real in a notion existed in God, the source of all reality" (1:395f.).

There is no need in the present context to examine Kant's argument critically. Nor do I want to focus on the subtle shifts made in the argument when he recasts it in *The One Possible Basis.*[5] Instead, let us turn directly to the first *Critique* and see how the argument appears in the light of Kant's critical position. It is in the Transcendental Dialectic, in the chapter on the Transcendental Ideal, that we find it taken up again.

In the middle of the Dialectic, Kant presents us with a new synthetic a priori principle, namely, that of a thoroughgoing determination of all things. As we have seen, according to Kant, we come to know an object by determining it, that is, by ascribing predicates to it.[6] The object is simply the bearer of certain predicates, a 'something in general' that we think to ourselves through the predicates that constitute its concept. In principle, however, the object must also be determin*able* with respect to the predicates that were not asserted or denied of it. The determinateness of the object precludes the possibility that any predicate may, at one and the same time, apply and not apply to it. Or, as Kant says, "every thing, as regards its possibility, is . . . subject to the principle of thoroughgoing determination, according to which if all the possible predicates of things be taken together with their contradictory opposites, then one of each pair of contradictory opposites must belong to it" (A571f.).

This principle rests on what Kant calls a necessary "transcendental presupposition," namely, the idea of an *omnitudo realitatis*, of a "transcendental substrate" that contains, as it were, "the whole store of material" for all possible predicates of things. His reasoning is by now familiar. We cannot think of a finite thing except in terms of some limitation or privation. But a limitation, as a determination of an object, is always derivative and presupposes the thought of the realities that it limits and that contain the data or material for the possibility and thoroughgoing determination of the thing: "All manifoldness of things is only a correspondingly varied mode of limiting the concept of the highest reality which forms their common substratum, just as all figures are only possible as so many different modes of limiting infinite space" (A578).

We are thus led by reason to form the idea of an object that, although transcendent, is regarded as being thoroughly determinable in accordance with principles. In other words, we form an *ideal,* by which Kant understands an idea, "not merely *in concreto,* but *in individuo,* that is, as an individual thing" (A568), determined or determinable by the idea alone.

At this point, Kant radically breaks with his earlier thought. In order to represent to ourselves the thoroughgoing determinateness of things, we need not presuppose the *existence* of a being that corresponds to this ideal, but only the *idea* of such a being. That is to say, to derive the conditioned totality, "the totality of the limited," from an unconditioned totality of thoroughgoing determination, we require not the objective relation of an actual object to other things, but only of "an idea to concepts" (A578f.). Owing to a natural illusion, however, we confound what is a subjective condition of thought with an objective condition of things in general. The first step is innocent enough. For an object of sense to be thoroughly determined, it must be compared with all predicates that can be given in the field of appearances. Now, whatever is real in the field of appearances is given in experience, which is inevitably "considered as single and all-embracing" (A582), for there is only "one single experience in which all perceptions are represented as in thoroughgoing and orderly connection" (A110), just as there is only one space and one time in which appearances can occur. The material for the possibility of all objects of the senses must thus be presupposed as given in one *Inbegriff* or whole, upon whose limitation the determination of all things and their distinction from one another must be based (see A581f.). But now, neglecting the distinction between appearances and things in themselves, we confound the unity that is merely given as a task *(aufgegeben)* with one that could be given as such:

> We substitute dialectically for the *distributive* unity
> of the empirical employment of the understanding,
> the *collective* unity of experience as a whole; and
> then think this whole [realm] of appearances as one

> single thing that contains all empirical reality in it-
> self; and then again, in turn, by means of . . . [a]
> transcendental subreption, substitute for it the con-
> cept of a thing which stands at the source of the
> possibility of all things, and supplies the real condi-
> tions for their complete determination. (A582f.)

If we were entitled to substitute the *collective* unity of experience as a whole for the *distributive* unity of the empirical employment of the understanding (as Kant had done in his
earlier writings) and thus to hypostatize what is available to
us only as an idea, we would indeed, Kant points out, "be
able to determine the primordial being through the mere concept of the highest reality, as a being that is one, simple, all-
sufficient, eternal," that is, God (A580). Such an assertion
cannot be warranted, however, and the aspirations of transcendental theology are curtailed once and for all. The idea of
a supreme being, according to the critical Kant, remains "an
ideal without a flaw" (A641), but its true epistemic function
is only that of a regulative principle of reason that allows us
to look upon all connection in the world *as if* it originated
from an all-sufficient necessary cause, and to base on the idea
of such a cause the rule of a systematic and necessary unity
explaining that connection (see A619). But this ideal of a
supreme being, as presented in the Dialectic, specifies no particular rule for the thoroughgoing determination of all things;
it signifies the goal for our investigation—nothing further.

Ether Proof

This is not yet Kant's last word on the *omnitudo realitatis*. In
the *Opus postumum* we encounter another version of it, in the
form of his ether proofs. The sudden appearance of these
proofs, in the sheets "Übergang 1–14" of early 1799, is alto-

gether surprising and at first difficult to understand. Kant now no longer regards the ether as a hypothesis for explaining certain physical phenomena but deduces it from the conditions of possible experience. In the previous chapters we saw that Kant, in the early sketches of the *Opus postumum*, introduced the ether or caloric to explain the possibility of particular properties of matter, most important cohesion, and to account for the formation of material bodies from an originally fluid state. We also noted his attempts, thus far by and large unfruitful, to develop an elementary system of the moving forces of matter from the table of categories in conjunction with the assumption of such a universally distributed world-matter. Only toward the end of 1798, on the last pages of the drafts "Elem. Syst. 1–7," does Kant succeed in carrying the classification of the moving forces of matter through all the four functions of the categories and assign the ceaseless agitations of the ether itself to the function of modality (category of necessity).

It is at this point that I want to take up again Kant's reflections where we had left them in Chapter 1 and continue the closer examination of the unfolding of his argument. Kant has by now firmly established that all mechanical forces of matter depend for their possibility on the dynamical forces of the ether, and thus all parts of matter distributed in space are interrelated as members of a universal mechanical system of the forces which originally and constantly (according to modality) agitate matter. Kant lists this as the "Postulate of Dynamics" and adds in the margin: "The collective idea of all the moving forces of matter precedes a priori the distributive idea of all the particular forces, which are only empirical" (22:200, Op. 55). Soon thereafter, Kant applies this thought to the Transition itself. The Transition "is itself a system which contains a priori the form of the system of physics. What contains the possibility of physics as a whole cannot be a fragmentary aggregate; for, as a whole given a priori, it must necessarily be a system which is capable neither of increase

nor of diminution. Regulative principles which are also constitutive" (22:241, Op. 57).

These statements seem to be prima facie in conflict with
the position of the first *Critique* that I have just sketched. Before going any further, therefore, let us see if Kant now indeed contradicts anything of what he established in 1781. A
dialectical illusion will inevitably arise, Kant argued in the
Dialectic of the *Critique of Pure Reason,* if we substitute for
the distributive unity of the empirical employment of the understanding the collective unity as a whole and think of this
whole realm of appearances as one single existing thing. The
distributive unity that the understanding achieves can only
yield an aggregate of perceptions; it cannot constitute a system of experience. It was the task of the ideas of reason, in
their regulative employment, to bring as much systematic
unity as possible into the manifold of empirical concepts,
"positing a certain collective unity as a goal of the activities of
the understanding, which otherwise are concerned solely
with distributive unity" (A644). Reason does so by project-
ing a certain point—a *focus imaginarius*—toward which it di-
rects all the efforts of the understanding, a point where these
efforts might converge as upon their point of intersection.
The concepts of the understanding do not of course proceed
from this point, but they gain the greatest possible unity and
extension by being directed toward this goal.

In the *Opus postumum* this perspective is reversed, the
focus imaginarius now being also the principle from which
the systematic unity of all the moving forces of matter is
thought to emerge. The principle of a formal purposiveness
of nature that Kant had discovered subsequent to the first
Critique (and that I discussed in Chapter 1) led to an expanded view of nature, of nature as itself systematic and purposive, not simply a blind mechanism. If nature, for the sake
of judgment, specifies its empirical laws to the form of a system, then the collective unity of its forces must precede the

distributive unity of the perceptions of them. And it was precisely this realization of a formal purposiveness of nature that convinced Kant that a Transition to physics was possible and indeed required: a Transition, to wit, that provides physics with "the sketch of a system" for the investigation of nature's own systematic unity. For a system is the unity of the manifold modes of knowledge under one idea—the idea of the form of the whole that determines a priori both the scope of its manifold elements and the positions that they occupy relative to one another. The unity of a system is thus always collective, a connection of its parts in conformity with a single principle. If physics is the systematic study of nature, the idea of nature as a collective whole of moving forces must lie at the basis of its investigation; this idea, however, physics cannot gain from an empirical aggregate of perceptions but must receive from the Transition. The Transition must itself be systematic to provide physics with "the sketch of a system," and it must derive its own systematicity from the idea of a collective whole of nature's moving forces. In other words, the Transition must be based on a principle that is both regulative and constitutive: by anticipating regulatively the whole of nature, the Transition must develop the systematic principle that is constitutive of physics as a system. "There is a not merely regulative, but also constitutive formal principle, existing a priori, of the science of nature, for the purpose of a system" (22:240, Op. 56; see also 22:312.4f.).

There is still no indication in these sheets prior to "Übergang 1–14" that Kant knew how the idea of a collective unity of the moving forces of matter can provide the Transition with its long-sought principle. Transition and ether each seem to depend on the other for an account of their own systematic nature, and it appears that Kant has not yet advanced significantly over his earlier descriptions of his Transition project. Then, beginning in April 1799 with draft "Übergang 2," Kant suddenly adopts an entirely new strategy and gives his project a new direction: he now begins to deduce the actuality of the ether or caloric from the conditions of possible experience. The proof is striking in many ways; for a start it might be best to cite a few passages at length.

> If it can be proved that the unity of the *whole* of possible experience rests upon the existence of such a material [i.e., ether] (with its stated properties), then its actuality is also proved, not, indeed, *through* experience, but a priori, merely from conditions of *possibility,* for the sake of the possibility of experience . . . Now the concept of the whole of outer experience . . . presupposes all possible moving forces of matter as combined in collective unity; to wit, in full space (for empty space, be it space enclosed within bodies or surrounding them externally, is not an object of possible experience). It further presupposes, however, a constant *motion* of all matter, by which the *subject,* as an object of sense, is affected. For without this motion, that is, without the stimulation of the sense organs, which is its effect, no perception of any object of the senses, and hence no experience, takes place. (22:550–551, Op. 86–87)

> The principle which serves as the basis for the combination of all moving forces of matter into a whole of all possible experience is the assumption of a material which is uniformly distributed throughout cosmic space, and which penetrates all bodies internally. (21:540.24–27)

> The object of an all-embracing experience contains within it all the subjectively moving forces of matter (that is to say, those affecting the senses and producing perceptions). Their whole is called

caloric and is the basis of this universal stimulation of forces. (22:553, Op. 89)

Caloric is actual, because the concept of it (with the attributes we ascribe to it) makes possible the whole of experience; it is given by reason, not as a hypothesis for perceived objects, for the purpose of *explaining* their phenomena, but rather, immediately, in order to found the possibility of experience itself. (22:554, Op. 89)

All so-called *experiences* are always only parts of *one* experience, in virtue of the universally distributed, unbounded caloric which connects all celestial bodies in one system and sets them into a community of reciprocity. (22:554fn., Op. 89fn.)

At least three strands in these passages are important in the present context.[7] The first concerns the nature of perception. In the first *Critique,* Kant had defined perception as appearance combined with consciousness (A120); this definition is now expanded. For an appearance to count as a perception, I must be able to think that it arises in my consciousness because of the influence its object has exerted on my senses. Any perception of an outer object is also the effect of a moving force of matter on me.

The second strand connects with the problem of the Refutation of Idealism that I mentioned earlier: for experience of outer objects to be possible, space itself must be an object of sense. Since the space we encountered in the first *Critique,* the mere form of intuition, was "neither positively empty nor positively full, [hence] not an object existing outside myself at all" (21:232, Op. 78), space must now be thought of as filled with moving forces. The ether or caloric "makes space sensible"; it is "the hypostatized space itself, as it were, in which everything moves" (21:228, 224, Op. 76, 73). Kant thus calls the realization of space a condition of the possibility of experience in general, and it is no accident that, at one point, Kant gives the ether proof in the *Opus postumum* precisely the same form that he gave to the Refutation in the first *Critique*, that is, *Grundsatz* followed by *Beweis*, and then *Anmerkungen* that reflect on the method of proof (see 21:223–226, Op. 72–74).

The third strand, most significantly, unites the other two and connects with my discussion of Kant's transcendental ideal in the first *Critique*. Perceptions of outer objects are the effects of moving forces upon us; experience, by contrast, is knowledge by means of connected perceptions. If experience is also to be systematic, there must be a basis for combining all moving forces of matter into a single, all-embracing whole. The possibility of experience in this sense thus presupposes a collective unity of the forces from which the distributive unity of experience can be derived.

The actual text of the *Opus postumum* contains a remarkable number of attempted deductions of the ether, varying several of its elements and trying out ever new formulations. None of these versions seems to have satisfied Kant completely, for even in the amanuensis's copy of "Übergang 9–11" he subsequently crossed out the passages containing the ether proof (see 22:552–555, Op. 87–90). At the same time, the variations in these proofs are sufficiently minor so as to leave no doubt that Kant at this time thought it possible to deduce the actuality of an ether. To better understand his procedure, we must therefore sidestep these variations and try to reconstruct the essential structure of his proof from the various sketches.[8]

To begin with, Kant himself remarks several times that the proof consists of two stages or steps, one "subjective," the other "objective." The subjective step concerns the conditions of a possible unified experience. We must take care to note, however, that "unity of experience" is here understood not in the sense of the Analytic of the first *Critique*, as distributive unity in the progression of the synthesis of given representations in accordance with the categories, but as the collective unity of the experience of the moving forces affecting the subject. The objective step, by contrast, concerns the principle of nature's own systematic unity in its moving forces. Taken together, both steps aim at demonstrating that what is subjectively valid must also be objectively real or actual, in virtue of the principle of identity: "Hence, the material must be valid both subjectively, as the basis of the representation [of] the whole of an experience, and objectively, as a principle for the unification of the moving forces of matter" (22:554, Op. 89). The material in question is the ether or caloric, and the goal of the proof can hence be expressed in the following way: "If it can be proved that the unity of the *whole* of possible experience rests upon the existence of such a material (with its stated properties), then its actuality is also proved, not, indeed, *through* experience, but a priori, merely from conditions of *possibility,* for the sake of the possibility of experience" (22:550, Op. 86f.). Let us first look at the subjective side of Kant's ether proof, which might be reconstructed from the text as follows:

Subjective Step

P1 Experience is knowledge by means of connected perceptions (B161).
P2 Perceptions of outer objects are the effects of moving forces of matter on the perceiving subject (definition of perception).
P3 Space is essentially one (A25).

1 For experience to be possible, it is necessary that perceptions can be connected (from P1).
2 For experience to be possible, it is necessary that the effects of the moving forces of matter on the perceiving subject can be connected (from P2 and 1).

3 Empty space cannot be an object of perception (from P2 and concept of empty space).[9]

4 Perceptible space is essentially one (from P3 and 3).

5 Perceptible space must be thought as filled everywhere with moving forces (from P2 and 3).[10]

6 The space in which perceptions can be connected must be thought as filled everywhere with moving forces (from P1 and 5).

7 A single space filled everywhere with moving forces is a condition of the possibility of experience (from P1, 2, and 4).

8 Hence we form the idea of an elementary material[11] that

according to space is universally distributed and all-penetrating,[12] thus including within itself all other moving forces;

according to time is permanently moving, by its own attraction and repulsion alone, and that is originally moving all others.[13]

The object of this idea we call "ether" or "caloric."

9 *Conclusion:* "Thus the principle of this synthetic unity of the whole of the object of possible experience is merely *subjective* (a principle of *composition*—not of the possibility of what is composite, outside the representation of the object)" (21:583, Op. 91) (from 7 and 8).

The second, or "objective," step of the argument is harder to make out in the text. Most of its premises are only implied at this stage of the Transition. I offer the following as a reconstruction.

Objective Step

P4 We do have experience of outer objects (premise of the Transition).

[90]

P5 Nature is the complex *(Inbegriff)* of all things insofar as they can be objects of our senses and hence also objects of experience (*Metaphysical Foundations* 4:467).

P6 Nature, as the complex of all things insofar as they can be objects of our senses and hence also objects of experience, forms a system for our power of judgment (*Critique of Judgment* 5:246; cf. 20:213fn.).

P7 The form of a system consists in the necessary unity of its elements in conformity with a single principle (A645, 832f.).

P8 (1) The ether or caloric is a material distributed in cosmic space that can exist not as an aggregate of parts but only collectively, in the form of a system.[14]
(2) The ether or caloric is the *only* candidate for a material distributed in cosmic space that can exist not as an aggregate of parts but only collectively, in the form of a system.[15]

10 Nature consists in the necessary unity of its moving forces, in conformity with a single principle (from P1, P2, P6, P7).

11 The only candidate for a principle that unites all moving forces of nature into a collective whole is the ether or caloric (from P7, P8).

12 There exists outer experience, and hence nature as a collective whole of perceptions (from P4, P6).

13 *Conclusion:* "Caloric is actual, because the concept of it (with the attributes we ascribe to it) makes possible the whole of experience" (22:554, Op. 89) (from 11 and 12).[16]

What this conclusion means precisely, and especially what "attributes" we have to ascribe to the ether, will become clearer shortly. But first some comments on the status of the ether in this proof are in order. I suggest that the ether is best understood as a transcendental ideal in the critical sense.[17]

That is, it is the idea of an individual thing thoroughly determined or determinable by the idea alone. Kant makes this clear in a number of passages that reflect on the peculiar nature of the ether proof, for instance: "This mode of proving the existence of an outer sense-object must strike one as *unique* of its kind (without example); nevertheless, this should not appear strange, since its object also has the peculiarity that it is *individual* and . . . contains in itself *collective*, not merely *distributive* universality" (21:603, Op. 96). Again, "This *indirect* proof is *unique* of its kind—a fact that should not appear strange, since what it concerns is an *individual* object, which carries with it real (not logical) *universality*" (21:586, Op. 93). Finally, "The object of a single, all-embracing experience is, at the same time, an individual *(individuum)*" (22:611, Op. 98).

The second feature of a Kantian ideal that is of importance in this context is that although the object of an ideal cannot be given in experience, it must not be regarded as a fantasy, or as a figment of the imagination. Ideals have practical power as regulative principles and function as the 'basis' of a possible perfection of certain actions, such as the thoroughgoing determination of experience: "Reason, in its ideal, aims . . . at complete determination in accordance with a priori rules. Accordingly, it thinks for itself an object which it regards as being completely determinable in accordance with principles" (A571).

In calling Kant's ether an ideal, I do not want to deny that Kant may have wavered—for a while at least—in his assessment of the status of the ether. At some places, for instance, Kant says that for the ether, and for it alone, *"a posse ad esse valet consequentia"* (21:592.11; cf. 21:604f., Op. 97). The ether thus exists "outside the idea" of it (21:559.19). At other places, however, it is said to exist only "in idea" (21:553, Op. 82), and to be merely "a thought-object *(ens rationis)*" (21:231, Op. 77). But whether this ambivalence merely reflects different emphases of the two sides of his proof (subjective and objective) or indicates a genuine uncertainty as to the ether's actual existence I want to leave undecided for now. I do favor the first alternative, and for the purpose of my interpretation, I take a statement such as the following to express Kant's position adequately:

> Now what is at issue in the question whether there is an all-penetrating etc. *elementary material* is the subjective element of receptivity to the sense-object, [which is required] for this material to be the object of a synthetic-universal experience; it is not whether the material exists *in itself* with those attributes. It is a matter of whether the empirical intuition of the elementary material, as belonging to the whole of a possible experience, already contains these attributes in its concepts (according to the principle of identity)—an issue which relates solely to the cognitive faculty, insofar as this faculty contains in idea the whole of possible experience in one total representation (and so must think of it as given a priori). Hence, the material must be valid both subjectively, as the basis of the representation [of] the whole of an experience, and objectively, as a principle for the unification of the moving forces of matter. (22:554, Op. 89)[18]

There is, however, another reason why ether proofs and transcendental ideal could, and should, be linked. This reason concerns the often noted (yet never explained) fact that, whereas changes in Kant's position in the *Opus postumum* usually occur gradually and over a traceable period of time, the shift in his ether theory—from a merely hypothetical to an a priori demonstrable material—takes place suddenly and without warning. This rather dramatic shift occurs on the seventh sheet of the second fascicle, which, fortunately, we can date fairly precisely. At the end of the sheet there is a reference to J. G. Herder's *Verstand und Erfahrung: Eine Metakritik zur Kritik der reinen Vernunft,* which came out in late April or early May 1799.[19] The new reflections on the ether that precede this remark are thus likely to date from the previous days or weeks (that is, March or April 1799). At that time, might an external event have contributed to Kant's change of mind?

In 1797, with Kant's permission, Johann Heinrich Tieftrunk, a professor at Halle and a mediator in Kant's growing difficulties with J. S. Beck, had taken on the task of producing an edition of Kant's shorter works. Kant had offered to write a preface to this edition that "would express my approval not only of your bringing the book out but also of any commentary you might be adding" (12:240). He requested only that the volumes be sent to him prior to publication. Tieftrunk complied with Kant's wishes on March 12, 1799, pointing out that he had appended to Kant's works occasional commentary "for the convenience of the reader" (13:510). He also explained that he would need Kant's preface by the end of April for it to be included in the edition. Mail from Halle to Königsberg took about a week in those days, so Kant would have examined Tieftrunk's edition and his annotations in late March or early April 1799.

One piece of commentary by Tieftrunk seems especially important in the present context; it is almost seventeen pages long and is appended to Kant's 1763 essay *The One Possible Basis for a Demonstration of God's Existence.*[20] In it, Tieftrunk discusses the relation between this work and Kant's treatment of rational theology in the first *Critique.* Again, there is an external reason for such a lengthy and detailed commentary. Only five years earlier (1794), a new edition of *The One Possible Basis* had appeared—the first after the critical works. Naturally, it had invited a comparison of Kant's treatment of proofs for God's existence in the texts of 1763 and 1781. There is an astonishing discrepancy between the two works that is hard to overlook.

Kant concludes *The One Possible Basis* by saying that there are four possible ways in which one might try to prove God's existence, that is (in his later terminology), the ontological, the cosmological, the physico-theological, and his own proof from the ground of all possibility. Whereas the first two are doomed to failure, the third has emotional appeal but cannot serve as a proof. This leaves his own argument as the only possible proof. In the Dialectic of the first *Critique,* however, Kant claimed that "there are only three possible ways of proving the existence of God by means of speculative reason"—the ontological, the cosmological, and the physico-theological—and concluded that none of them could in principle succeed: "There are, and there can be, no others" (A591). His own proof of 1763 was not even mentioned, and it was thus natural to assume that Kant, in the first *Critique,* had not really succeeded in showing the impossibility of rational theology *as such,* and that there was still a "possible basis" for a proof of its supreme being. Such a view, incidentally, was expressed soon after the publication of Kant's *Critique,* for example, in J. A. H. Ulrich's *Institutiones Logicae et Metaphysicae* of 1785, and by Moses Mendelssohn, who in his *Morgenstunden* of the same year offered just such *Beweisgründe* for God's existence again.[21]

Tieftrunk tried to meet this charge in his commentary on Kant's pre-critical essay by suggesting that Kant's 1763 proof of God's existence was fundamentally identical with, although an improved form of, the ontological argument.[22] This solution would hardly have met with Kant's approval, yet in April or May 1799 it brought again to Kant's attention his discussion of the transcendental ideal, as well as his earlier argument for the existence of a being whose theoretical function was very similar to that which he now wanted to ascribe to the ether. It is easy to see why Kant could have thought that this argument might now be used more profitably. When presenting his original proof for God's existence, Kant did not yet distinguish between the unconditional necessity of judgments and the absolute necessity of things. From the fact that we cannot think anything as possible unless the predicates to be compared are available, Kant concluded that the realities we think in these predicates must themselves exist with absolute necessity. Only in the second half of the 1760s was Kant able to penetrate the illusion involved here and realize that no contradiction can result from thinking the nonexistence of a being, no matter what that being is.[23] This, of course, was the decisive move. From that moment on, ontotheology had to become a non-discipline, because all theoretical proofs for God's existence could now be seen as having the same chances of success as, say, constructions of a *perpetuum mobile*. An ether proof, however, would not have to be affected by the same problem. For it is not the absolute necessity of the ether as such that Kant wanted to establish, but only its necessity for a possible unified experience. We *can* after all think the non-existence of the ether, unlike that of Kant's pre-critical God.[24] For this very reason, the old argument must suddenly have seemed endowed with new and unforeseen promise.

And at first glance, Kant's ether proofs do indeed bear an interesting resemblance to his earlier proofs for God's existence. One structural similarity in particular sheds light on the peculiar nature of his ether proofs. That is to say, Kant never doubted that, if God's existence as *omnitudo realitatis* could be proved (which it cannot), we would also be able to determine his essential attributes—analytically, and according to the table of categories—from the mere concept of the highest reality: "as a being that is one, simple, all-sufficient, eternal" (A580; cf. 2:81–97). Similarly, Kant suddenly realized, if the ether can be assigned the status of an ideal, we must likewise be in a position to determine *its* attributes analytically, from its mere concept, in virtue of its function as the ground of all realities:

> The attributes of this [material] (since it is all-embracing, *individual* [*unica*] and the basis of all [forces] for the unity of the object of the one experience) are given according to the principle of identity: namely, that it is *universally distributed, all-penetrating,* and *all-moving* . . . And as such, it is necessary, that is, *permanent.* For *sempernitas est necessitas phaenomenon.* (21:584, Op. 92)

More precisely, since the ether is all-embracing and individual *(unica),* it must be universally distributed (Quantity). In order to serve as the basis for the combination of all moving forces of matter, it must be all-penetrating (Quality). Since its inner oscillations are said to be the condition of the formation of bodies, it must be all-moving (Relation). And since the unity of experience permits no interruptions, the internal motions of the ether must be permanent, that is, necessary (Modality). To this Kant adds soon thereafter:

> This matter [the ether] is also, as a consequence of the aforementioned attributes, negatively characterized: as imponderable, incoercible, incohesible and inexhaustible . . . Ponderability, coercibility, cohesion and exhaustibility presupposes moving forces which act in opposition to the latter and cancel their effect. (22:610, Op. 98)

It is not hard to imagine why even Kant's handwriting (according to Adickes) now shows signs of renewed hope. Although the ether is a non-empirical material and as such transcendent, it must be possible, in virtue of the collective universality it contains, to demonstrate its actuality, if only indirectly, from the conditions of possible experience. More important, however, if the actuality of this material is demonstrable, then the elementary system of the moving forces of matter can be developed from the concept of this ether. Since all objects of outer sense depend on moving forces that limit the original force continuum, the physicist must investigate them systematically and try to determine their degree, through observation and experiments. This is possible, however, only if the understanding previously "inserts" *(hinein-legen)* the elementary concepts of the Transition into the sensible representations for the possibility of experience. The principle of the Transition, Kant points out, must be a schema of the combination of the moving forces "in conformity with the schema of the Analogies of Experience" (22:375, Op. 119). And of the concepts of 'substance' and 'causality' he has also shown that "we can extract clear concepts of them from experience, only because we have inserted them into experience, and because experience is thus itself brought about only by their means" (A196). Accordingly, Kant writes on sheet "N" of the tenth fascicle:

> The transition to physics does not come about through what sense in empirical intuition (perception) *extracts from* experience, for in that case it would remain entirely undetermined what and how much may be given for our sense-representation. Rather it comes about through what the understanding *inserts into* the sense-representation *for the sake of* experience and its possibility, for a system of [experience] and its possible unity. [It comes about] through what the understanding *inserts* according to the categories of *Quantity* (ponderable or not), *Quality* (coercible or not), *Relation* (cohesible or not), and *Modality* (exhaustible or not) in order to underlay [*unterlegen*] the object of empirical intuition with a system of perceptions, through concepts of the relations of the moving forces.

[98]

(22:378.26–379.1; see also 22:325, Op. 109, and so on)

Thus the ether proof provides Kant with the "sketch of a system" that must precede the scientific investigation of nature; it provides the "topic of the moving forces of matter" (21:487, Op. 44) in which specific, empirical forces of nature can be assigned their location. The concept of the ether as "the concept of *unity* of the thoroughgoing combination of matter," Kant now realizes, "necessarily presents, although only in idea, an *elementary system* of the moving forces of matter" (21:539.6–9). Accordingly, the existence of the ether or caloric is heralded, especially in the paragraph headings of the text, as "The Supreme *Principle* of the Elementary System of the Moving Forces of Matter" (21:591.2–4; see also 589, Op. 94, and 269 note 59).

And we can now see more clearly how both steps of the ether proof interlock to establish the result that is needed for the Transition: when regarded subjectively as perceptible space, the ether is a condition of the combination of outer perceptions into the whole of possible experience; when regarded objectively as the principle of nature's systematic unity, and of one collective experience, the ether is an ideal whose attributes provide the Elementary System with its fundamental concepts. Thus it is no accident that Kant in these proofs speaks of the ether "with its stated properties" (22:550, Op. 86) and "with the attributes we ascribe to it" (22:554, Op. 89), rather than of the ether simpliciter. It is precisely these properties or attributes that make possible the a priori classification of the moving forces of matter in the Transition from the metaphysical foundations of natural science to physics.

Once this result is established, Kant begins new sheets on which he composes the first chapters of the long-delayed book on the Transition; then he has an (unknown) amanuen-

sis make fair copies of them (see 22:543–555, Op. 82–90)—
usually the last step before a manuscript is sent to the
publisher or printer.[25] The fundamental problem of the Transition is solved, the 'idea' on which to base it has been found,
and the elementary system of the moving forces of matter, so
far as such a system is possible a priori, can finally be brought
to its conclusion. The principle of the possibility of a universally distributed caloric, as well as the necessity of its assumption, Kant explains, belong to the elementary system of
the moving forces; with the proof of its existence, however,
"the *doctrinal system* of the transition to physics (not the *system of nature*) can be concluded" (22:584.8).

Perhaps not quite yet. At least it seems that Kant, as soon
as he had found this solution to the problem of the Transition, clearly realized its insufficiency. Indeed, he had found a
principle for his elementary system and a topic for the classification of forces, but the problem of the *knowability* of the
moving forces of matter was not thereby solved. For specific
forces of nature cannot be cognized as it were passively,
through staring at them, nor by reflecting on their possible
manifestations in experience, but only through interacting
with them, in the to and fro of *actio* and *reactio*. In other
words, the subjective side of the ether proofs, the subject's
apprehension of sensible space and of the moving forces in it
that make it sensible, is still unclear philosophically. Thus
it is hardly surprising that by August 1799, Kant's ether
proofs ended as suddenly as they had surfaced only three
months earlier. Instead the question is now raised: *What is
physics?* which increasingly comes to mean *What does the
physicist do?*

This is how Kant describes the remaining problem: "The
topic of the moving forces of matter . . . does not yet, on
its own, found an experience" (22:356f., Op. 115). Instead,
this topic, once it has been "analytically investigated" *(auf-*

suchen), must be "synthetically presented" (22:299, Op. 103); that is, the physicist must *move* the object[26] and *insert* a priori into the appearances what she seeks to know systematically in them: "The transition to physics, consequently, is the predetermination *(praedeterminatio)* of the inner active relations of the subject that combines [*zusammenstellen*] perceptions to the unity of experience ... namely, [through] a principle of the a priori division of the moving forces according to their relations—as ponderable or imponderable, coercible or incoercible, cohesible or incohesible, finally as exhaustible or inexhaustible matter with its moving forces" (22:337.5–15). This thought sets the stage for the *Selbstsetzungslehre* of the later fascicles, to which I shall turn next.

Selbstsetzungslehre

This doctrine[27] is best approached systematically as much as historically. Again it will be advisable to start from the first *Critique,* more precisely, from Kant's claim that "the synthetic unity of apperception is ... that highest point to which we must ascribe all employment of the understanding" (B134).

Most important, the consciousness of myself in the representation 'I' is not an intuition but the mere awareness of the spontaneity of a thinking subject. That is to say, as Kant explicates, if I represent myself merely as subject of thought, whereby thought is taken by itself, as the pure spontaneity of the combination of the manifold of a merely possible intuition, I do not represent myself as appearance. And this is because thought as yet takes no account of the mode of intuition. In original self-consciousness, "I am conscious of myself, not as I appear to myself, nor as I am in myself, but only that I am. This representation is a *thought,* not an *intu-*

ition" (B157; see also B429). But this thought of myself would not exist, Kant argues, the act 'I think' could not take place, if nothing empirical were given as the condition of the application, or employment, of the pure intellectual faculty. For the 'I' of transcendental apperception has no existence independent of a synthesis of representations: as the principle of the combination of a manifold, it contains no manifold of its own for a possible synthesis. Consequently, I cannot just be the subject of thought; I am likewise aware of my existence, and the consciousness of myself must be viewed as involving an intuition, though one that as yet lacks determination. As Kant says: "The proposition, 'I think,' insofar as it amounts to the assertion, '*I exist thinking,*' is no mere logical function, but determines the subject (which is then at the same time object) in respect of existence" (B429). The 'I think', however, "precedes the experience which is required to determine the object of perception" (B423).

Kant's premise for the *Selbstsetzungslehre* of the *Opus postumum* is the same, though described differently. Again, we start with the act 'I think' as preceding all experience, the "mere logical function." The first act of spontaneity, Kant elaborates in various drafts especially of the seventh fascicle, is one of mere thinking. Because it does not yet involve any intuition, it is variously described as "logical" or "analytical" or as "explicative, according to the rule of identity" (cf. 22:420, Op. 184). It is analytical because it does not go beyond the mere thought of myself as such; it is explicative in that it lays bare what is involved in this thought, namely, that the I that thinks is an object of thought to itself: "The first act of the faculty of representation is the consciousness of myself through which the subject makes itself into an object" (22:77, Op. 186). And a few pages later: "The consciousness of myself *(apperceptio)* is the act of the subject to make itself into an object. It is merely logical *(sum)* without determination of the object *(apprehensio simplex)* . . . All cognition commences with the consciousness of myself; i.e., with representing myself, who is thinking (the subject), at the same time as object of this thinking" (22:89.15–25). The first act is not yet an act of the synthesis of a manifold (pure or given) but "the principle of the autonomy of making oneself into an object" (22:416, Op. 182). The task of the *Selbstsetzungslehre* is precisely to show how the I as mere object of thought *(cogitabile)* can become an empirical object given in space and time *(dabile)*.

No analytic unity of consciousness can be had without a synthetic unity. The act 'I think' could not take place if nothing were given to thought for its syntheses. This first act thus also implies the determin*ability* of myself as object, and the possibility to go beyond what Kant calls a merely logical self-consciousness. The second act must thus be a synthetic one. Moreover, it must be one that contains the conditions (at least some of them) for a further determination of myself, of the object of thought "in respect of existence." It must determine the forms under which something *can* be given to the spontaneity of thought. The second step "is ampliative, and goes beyond the given concept thereby that the subject *posits* itself in space- and time-relations, as pure (not empirical) intuitions . . . determining—not that which is itself object, but only the form of the intuition of the object" (22:420, Op. 184).

Of the details of this step Kant says little in the *Opus postumum,* but we can once again draw on the first *Critique* for further illustration of what he must have in mind. In the Transcendental Aesthetic, Kant had described sensibility, the forms of which are space and time, exclusively in terms of receptivity, as an altogether passive faculty. In both the first and second edition versions of the transcendental deduction of the categories, however, he introduced special arguments to clarify that space and time as formal intuitions presuppose a synthesis through which they can first be given as intuitions (see A99–102, B160–162fnn.). We cannot, he argues, even think a line without drawing it in thought, nor can we represent the three dimensions of Euclidean space except by setting three lines at right angles to one another from the same point. And it is by attending to the synthesis of a manifold, for instance, in the drawing of a straight line, that the concepts of 'succession' and of 'time' first become possible for us (see A99, B154).[28] It is the same spontaneous motion that the understanding also performs on any *given* manifold; here, however, this act is viewed by itself, apart from empirical intuition: "The understanding, under the title of a transcendental synthesis of imagination, performs this act on the *passive* subject, whose *faculty* it is, and we are therefore justified in saying that inner sense is affected thereby" (B153f.). Through such an act of transcendental motion or self-affection, a point emerges from which the lines are drawn and which the moving subject occupies. In addition, the forms emerge under which all objects must appear (namely, as simultaneous or successive, and, if they are to be distinguished from the subject and its various states, as outside and alongside one another). Of this Kant says in the *Opus postumum:* "Our sensible intuition is, initially, not perception (empirical representation with consciousness), for a principle of positing oneself and of becoming conscious of this position precedes it; and the form[s] of this positing of the manifold, as thoroughly combined, are the pure intuitions, which are called space and time (outer and inner intuition) and which, as unlimited according to concepts *(indefinita),* are represented in appearance as infinitely positive *(infinita)*" (22:420, Op. 184).

Up to this point, then, Kant's *Selbstsetzungslehre* can draw on the results of the first *Critique.* The question that arises next is how I am to proceed from here to empirical knowledge of myself as existing, as a corporeal being in a unified spatiotemporal experience. Since existence is not a real predicate, knowledge of my own existence can only consist in the thoroughgoing determination of the given manifold, and in the positing of a certain set of representations, united under the concepts of my empirical self, as outside that concept.

As the Refutation of Idealism had implied and Kant's ether proof aimed to establish, the next step in the determination of my own existence must be the realization of space as an object of sense. Space must be represented not merely as a formal intuition but as something existing outside me, as a totality of empirically identifiable locations. It can be this only if it is thoroughly filled with moving forces: "There must first be a matter filling space, ceaselessly self-moving by agitating forces (attraction and repulsion), before the location in space of every particle can be determined. This is the basis for any matter as object of possible experience" (21:550, Op. 81). The "hypostatization" of space, or the assumption of a universally distributed ether, is thus the third step in Kant's *Selbstsetzungslehre*.

But there must be more than a common basis of the moving forces of matter. For there to be experience of any particular object *in* space, the object's moving forces must affect the subject in order to be known as such. Perceptions of outer objects are not only "appearances combined with consciousness" (A120); they are likewise the effects of the agitating forces of matter on the subject. Before I can refer given representations to a common object, I must be able to think that object as exercising the forces on me that gave rise to the perception. Such forces, then, have likewise to be presupposed a priori for experience to be possible.

Setting aside for the moment the question of what forces must be thus presupposed, let us first ask how they are supposed to be known. Here Kant draws on a thought that is absent from his earlier works—a thought that gives his Transition project a completely new direction. Prima facie, it marks a continuation of the train of thought that was interrupted by Kant's occupation with Tieftrunk, and by his subsequent ether proofs. Immediately before the first occurrence of these proofs—on the same sheet, "Übergang 1"—Kant had pondered the question whether in the transition from the metaphysical foundations of natural science to physics there should be an a priori division of physical bodies into organic and inorganic bodies. Although the reality of organisms, that is, bodies in which all parts are reciprocally means and ends, cannot be guaranteed a priori, Kant argued that they have to be included, albeit only problematically (see 21:212, Op. 65), in the a priori division of bodies, because we are ourselves an example of organically moving forces and spontaneous intentional action. On the sheet immediately preceding the ether proofs, Kant writes: "The principle of the spontaneity of the motion of the parts of our own body (as limbs), considering the latter as our own self, is a mechanism"; and "Because man is conscious of himself as a self-moving machine, without being able to further understand such a possibility, he can, and is entitled to, introduce a priori organic-moving forces of bodies into the classification of bodies in general" (21: 212–213, Op. 65–66).

After the ether proofs, in fascicles 10 and 11, Kant capitalizes on this idea of an a priori consciousness of our own moving forces. Only because we ourselves exercise moving forces do we apprehend the appearances of moving forces upon us. But—and this is the crucial part of Kant's argument—only in the process of such apprehension can we, and do we, appear to ourselves as empirical beings. Empirical self-consciousness emerges at the point of intersection (interaction) between the moving forces of matter as they affect me, and my own motions thereon. That is to say, on the one hand, only because I am corporeal—a system of organically moving forces—can I be affected by moving forces of matter; on the other hand, only insofar as I can represent myself *as affected* do I *appear* to myself as sensuous and corporeal, that is, as an object of outer sense. Self-affection and affection through objects must thus be regarded as two sides of the

same coin: "Positing and perception, spontaneity and receptivity, the objective and subjective relation, are simultaneous;
because they are identical as to time, as appearances of how
the subject is *affected*—thus are given a priori in the same
actus" (22:466, Op. 132).

"Given a priori in the same *actus*" means that from this act
there originally emerges the duality of empirical self and material world surrounding it, of observer and observed. Only
because I apprehend the undetermined given manifold and, in
the process of apprehension, insert *(hineinlegen)* into it certain fundamental forces can I represent the manifold as the
appearance of an external cause of my perception, and at the
same time represent myself as being affected, and hence as
corporeal. "The subject affects itself and becomes an object in
appearance for itself in the composition of the moving
forces" (22:364.24–25).

This is Kant's general picture of how the next steps of the
Selbstsetzung must proceed. Can we spell out the details
more clearly? Trivially, the world we experience is a world
that fits our faculties and powers of cognition. The moving
forces I can become aware of initially will correspond to the
forces I am capable of exercising. But what are the forces of
attraction and repulsion that we exercise when moving—
forces that are also said to contain the key to the problem of a
"Transition from the metaphysical foundations of natural science to physics"?

In order to answer these questions, we may take our cue
from the following passage: "The moving forces of matter are
what the moving subject itself does with its body to [other]
bodies. The reactions corresponding to these forces are contained in the simple acts by which we perceive the bodies
themselves. Mechanics and dynamics are the two principles"
(22:326–327, Op. 110). What is meant by these two principles, mechanics and dynamics? Third, what are the "simple
acts" by which we perceive bodies?

MECHANICS. Quite generally, Kant characterizes mechanics in the *Opus postumum* as the art of using the moving forces of bodies, and of setting forces in motion by means of them. The bodies used for such purposes are called machines. Since antiquity, five (sometimes six) simple machines or "mechanical powers" were known to which all complex machines can be reduced. Kant usually reduces them further, though not consistently so, to lever, pulley, and inclined plane.[29] The forces directly set in motion by these mechanical powers are the attractive and repulsive forces of pressure (as in a lever), of traction (as in a pulley), and of shear (as in the case of an inclined plane on which a body slides).

Organisms, Kant had argued earlier, are complex natural machines. That is, they are physical objects equipped by nature with biological variations on the basic physical machines or powers. For example, higher-level organisms with hard skeletons rely heavily on compound lever systems (arms, legs), connected at low-friction fulcrums (knees, elbows), moved by muscles and biomechanical springs (tendons). Inclined planes in the form of wedges with sharpened edges serve many creatures as teeth, claws, or beaks. What distinguishes organisms from all other machines is that they also have the power of self-movement. Drawing on the works of Erasmus Darwin (1731–1802), John Brown (1735–1788), and Albrecht von Haller (1708–1777), Kant assigns to them animal (or vital) powers which function as the physiological basis for self-motion and for the reception and transmission of stimuli: nervous power as the principle of excitability (sensibility), and the power of muscular fiber as the ability to contract (irritability). The underlying idea is expressed with greater clarity in Schelling's *Ideas for a Philosophy of Nature* of 1797:

> The capacities of animal organs—sensibility, irritability, and the like—themselves presuppose an impulse principle, without which the animal would

be incapable of reacting to external stimulation, and only through this free reactivity of the organs does the stimulus from without become excitation and impression. Here the most complete reciprocity prevails: Only through excitation from without is the animal determined to movement, and conversely, only through this capacity to produce movement in itself does external impression become a stimulus. (Hence there can be neither irritability without sensibility nor sensibility without irritability.)[30]

This is now also Kant's view. Since human beings are one of nature's organisms, it perforce implies a modification of the theory of the Transcendental Aesthetic that goes beyond the supplementary arguments in the Deductions described above. For these arguments had left untouched sensibility's fundamental passivity[31] and only emphasized the need of a pure act of synthesis for the representation of space and time as formal intuitions. Kant's reasoning in the *Opus postumum,* by contrast, shows that sensibility cannot be described in terms of passivity alone. Something can be *given* to the subject only if it is received by a corresponding motion.[32] In other words, receptivity is only a relative form of passivity; it equally entails a reciprocal activity of the subject. Being reciprocal, the activity or motion in question must be subject to the same formal constraints as the receptivity to which it corresponds. Thus we find Kant now characterizing space and time not simply as forms of our intuition, as he had done in the first *Critique,* but as "forms of our effective forces [*Formen unserer Wirkungskräfte*]" (21:38.14); space and time are also forms of the forces by which I move and react to affection of the senses.[33] If the pure motion of the productive imagination underlies the space of geometry, organic self-motion must underlie all experience of the moving forces of matter, and hence the "hypostatization" of space as an object of the senses.

As a self-moving *machine,* however, I am endowed not only with animal powers but also with mechanical powers that I can, at least in part, use as instruments to exert motions and thereby elicit corresponding reactions. I can use the levers, springs, and inclined planes of my body to pull and push, to break and tear, to lift and throw, to mention just a few examples. Inexplicably, my body is both a natural object and thus subject to the laws of nature, *and* something that is subject, at least in part, to my *Willkür* and intentions. Kant expresses this point by saying that I am conscious of myself as a self-moving machine, "without being able to further understand such a possibility" (21:213, Op. 66). I become conscious of myself as a self-moving machine in the process of interacting with other bodies and of "inserting" forces into the yet undetermined manifold.

DYNAMICS. Machines, natural as well as artificial, presuppose for their possibility cohesion and solidity: the lever must resist breaking, the cord must not tear, the inclined plane must resist deformation. The same is true of the muscles, bones, fibers, and tendons of my own organism. Cohesion and solidity, however, depend in turn on the ceaseless agitations of an all-penetrating matter: the mechanics of moving forces is possible only under the presupposition of the dynamical forces of the ether. But this ether, Kant thinks, also sustains the vital polarity of nervous and muscular powers and unites "both forces into active and reactive, constantly alternating, play." That is why Kant adds to the two animal powers of excitability and irritability a third power, "a force which preserves all the organic forces of nature as a constant alteration of the former two, of which *one* phenomenon is heat" (22:300, Op. 103; cf. 22:301, Op. 104). And of this caloric he claims in his ether proof: "Caloric is actual, because the concept of it (with the attrib-

utes we ascribe to it) makes possible the whole of experience"
(22:554, Op. 89).

We can now see how Kant's argument must continue. The
third step of the *Selbstsetzungslehre* was the realization of
space, and thus the assumption of a universally distributed
ether. But it is not the mere thought of a force-continuum as
such that lets us progress beyond this step; it is the concept (or
ideal) of the ether *"with the attributes we ascribe to it"* that is
said to make possible the whole of experience. These attributes, as we have seen, can be enumerated analytically and in accordance with the table of categories. Negatively expressed,
the ether must be imponderable, incoercible, incohesible, and
inexhaustible. For there to be an experienceable item in space,
consequently, we must presuppose a priori limitations of the
original force continuum—limitations that constitute an object of experience and that the subject will have to investigate in
order to proceed in its thoroughgoing determination. In this it
must be guided by an a priori *topic* for the empirical forces,
based on the analytic determination of the attributes of the
ether in accordance with the system of categories. That is to
say: with regard to quantity, all matter must be either ponderable or imponderable; with regard to quality, either coercible
or incoercible; with regard to relation, cohesible or incohesible; and with regard to modality, exhaustible or inexhaustible.
Hence, the fourth step of the *Selbstsetzungslehre* must be the
Hineinlegen or insertion of these concepts into the sensible but
as yet undetermined manifold, to determine whether and to
what extent (in what degrees) they are instantiated in experience: "For we would have no consciousness of a hard or soft,
warm or cold, etc. body, *as such,* had we not previously formed
for ourselves the concept of these moving forces of matter (of
attraction and repulsion, or of extension and cohesion, which
we subordinate to them) and thus can say that one or the other
of these [properties] falls under such a concept" (22:341,
Op. 110–111).

THE SIMPLE ACTS. This leaves for the fifth step the execution of bodily motions, that is, motions of apprehension
and of the combination of forces that the subject initiates, in
accordance with the aforementioned four pairs of concepts of
the elementary system. "The four mechanical powers are the
moving forces of apprehension and reciprocal reaction. There
are four acts by which the subject affects itself as object and
thinks itself an object in appearance into a system of empirical representations, by means of perceptions of action, and
the reaction corresponding to it" (22:508, Op. 149). By exercising these acts, and by experiencing the corresponding reactions upon them, the subject originally becomes aware of
itself as affected, and thereby as a corporeal being in space to
which other things are external. This, then, is the last step in
the process Kant calls "self-positing." But these very acts—
and this, for Kant, is the key to the problem of the Transition—also lie at the bottom of any empirical knowledge of
objects and thus provide the a priori topoi for a scientific investigation of nature. "Only because the subject [is con-
scious] to itself of its moving forces (of agitating them)
and—because in the relationship of this motion, everything is
reciprocal—[is conscious] of perceiving a reaction of equal
strength (a relation which is known a priori, independently
of experience) are the counteracting moving forces of matter
anticipated and its properties established" (22:506, Op. 148).

To be sure, more cannot be determined a priori. We can en-
list the disjunctions of the elementary system analytically;
thereafter we must progress synthetically and empirically.
That is, the determination of the degree to which an object of
outer sense exemplifies one of these attributes has to be a
matter of experience. The Transition, after all, is a transition
to physics, not itself physics. The *Selbstsetzungslehre* determines my own existence, "but merely as appearance a priori"
(22:73.12). The essential point is that the subject has been
provided with an a priori guideline for the investigation of

nature and a principle that permits a first step in the thoroughgoing determination of its own existence in relation to the systematic unity of experience: "In the *transition* from the metaphysical foundations of natural science to physics nothing further is required than to make clear (and to develop a priori) what [these] concept[s] . . . contain in [themselves], and which of their consequences can be confirmed [*belegen*] with examples from experience (by means of observation and experiment)" (22:566.22–27).

Selbstsetzungslehre, ether theory, and the elementary system of the moving forces of matter thus hang together inextricably. I must posit myself as object in order to know myself as subject. The understanding as spontaneity subjects itself to the imperative *nosce te ipsum*—know thyself (see 22:22.9)—and proceeds by making itself into an object, and by bringing this object under concepts gained in the thoroughgoing determination of the sensible manifold. The determination of my own existence takes place for Kant within the context of the ideal of a single, all-embracing experience, itself depending on the collective unity of moving forces of matter, which the subject investigates, guided by the table of categories, progressing to a thorough determination of all phenomena. This process is never completed but inevitably given as a task: "The understanding begins with the consciousness of itself *(apperceptio)* and performs thereby a logical act. To this the manifold of outer and inner intuition attaches itself serially, and the subject makes itself into an object in a limitless sequence" (22:82, Op. 189).

If we now return once more to the problem discussed in Chapter 3, namely, the question of a "gap" in Kant's critical philosophy, another aspect of the *Selbstsetzungslehre* presents itself in a clearer light. For it has meanwhile emerged that although the concept of an object of outer sense cannot be constructed within the dynamical theory of matter, any "something that is to be an *object* of external sense" (and not just matter in general) must fall under the four functions of the categories *and* also fall under the four corresponding disjunctions of the Elementary System. Moreover, it has also emerged that I could not become empirically conscious of myself, and of myself as object, if I did not determine the degree to which what is to be an object of external sense exemplifies the attributes expressed in these categorial disjunctions. *Selbstsetzung* thus provides the *schema* for outer sense, the condition under which something can be given as object, or "the sensible concept, of an object in agreement with the category" (A146). Hence it fills the gap in Kant's critical philosophy.

Let us briefly review the path that has led us from the *Metaphysical Foundations of Natural Science* to the theoretical *Selbstsetzungslehre* of Kant's *Opus postumum*. Initially, this path took its course from two separate but related claims Kant made with regard to physics as a science of nature.

1. In 1786 Kant had insisted that every science that deserves this name must exhibit two essential features: (1) apodictic certainty with respect to its basic laws; and (2) systematic unity with respect to its manifold elements. Regarding (1), the *Metaphysical Foundations* had tried to show how the concept of the object of outer sense in general, matter, can be constructed in an a priori intuition. With regard to (2), it had carried the concept of matter through the four functions of the table of categories. Beyond that, Kant thought in 1786, philosophy cannot reach: the specific varieties of matter do not permit of a construction; they can only be "thought arbitrarily" *(willkürlich)* and listed accordingly, though without any a priori guarantee of completeness. Yet this remains unsatisfactory from the point of view of the systematicity of physics. For it was clear to Kant even at this time that physics cannot gain its systematicity empirically, any more than the apodictic certainty in its fundamental laws.

2. We noticed a change in Kant's position with respect to (2) sometime between the years 1787 and 1790: the discovery of the principle of reflective judgment provides an a priori justification to think of nature as itself systematic in its empirical laws. For this principle states that nature specifies its universal laws to empirical ones, according to the form of a system, for the sake of our power of judgment. Here we find the origin of Kant's Transition project: "Judgment first makes it possible, indeed necessary, for us to think of nature as having not only a mechanical necessity but also a purposiveness; if we did not presuppose this purposiveness, there could not be systematic unity in the thoroughgoing classification of particular forms in terms of empirical laws" (20:219). Yet this principle of a formal purposiveness only sets the stage for a possible Transition; none of the specific varieties of matter can be derived from it. There thus has to be a 'principle' of the Transition, or an 'idea' in accordance with which their basic forms can be thought, not voluntarily and arbitrarily but systematically.

3. By 1792 Kant seems to have developed doubts with regard to his earlier solution to (1), the construction of the concept of matter, as we witnessed in his letter to Beck. He speaks of a circle in his theory of matter that he does not yet know how to escape. First attempts can be seen to replace gravitational attraction in the dynamical model of matter with attraction in contact, or cohesion. With regard to (2), no new developments are observable.

4. In 1798 the revised theory of the formation of material bodies in terms of repulsion and cohesion is seen to be no longer constructible. Because of the importance of such a construction for the transcendental position of the first *Critique*, Kant now speaks of a "gap" in his critical philosophy. Regarding (2), no general principle for the classification of nature's moving forces has been discovered yet. What has become clear is that the a priori principle for such a classifica-

tion has to be gained in relation to the concept of a universally distributed ether or caloric.

5. In 1799 Kant is convinced that the idea of the ether as the material condition of a single unified experience also provides the long-sought principle for the Transition. To this end it must be treated like an *ideal* in the critical sense, as an individual determined and determinable by the idea alone. The "attributes we must ascribe to it" in virtue of its function provide the Elementary System of the moving forces with its fundamental concepts. In numerous attempts Kant tries to prove the objective reality of the ether by deducing its actuality from the conditions of a possible unified experience. These attempts come to an end when Kant realizes that knowing the topoi of the Elementary System does not suffice for a systematic cognition of the moving forces of matter: we must also be able to "insert" into the manifold of sense what we seek to extract from experience. This makes necessary an investigation of the self-constitution of the subject of knowledge as an object of experience. Here the concepts of the Elementary System finally gain their objective validity by being shown to be integral elements in the *Selbstsetzung* of the subject of experience.

This leaves a final question to be addressed: the unity of theoretical and practical reason. For I am not just a physical organism, an object of outer sense, but also a person who has rights and duties. How are both these elements connected from the standpoint of *Selbstsetzung?* Is there such a thing as practical self-positing as well?

CHAPTER FIVE

The Subject as Person
and the Idea of God

Kant's account of practical self-positing in the last two fascicles of the *Opus postumum* gives rise to interpretive problems that differ from those encountered in the previous chapters. Oddly, it seems to be not so much the initial strangeness of Kant's argumentation that complicates its comprehension as the overall familiarity of what he presents us with. Prima facie, the text appears to confirm our expectation that we already know from his earlier writings what it takes for a rational animal to constitute itself as a person: moral autonomy and the ability of pure reason to determine the will. What makes us persons in the Kantian sense is that we are agents whose reason can be practical of itself and be motivated by nothing but respect for the moral law.[1] No external incentive is required or even permitted for actions done from respect for the moral law: I subordinate my will to a law of which I myself am the author but that is nevertheless binding as a categorical imperative for every finite rational being endowed with a will.

This view, familiar from Kant's earlier writings, is also prevalent in the *Opus postumum*. At the same time, there are passages that seem hard to reconcile with this picture and that may cast a perplexing doubt on the purity of the moral principle. For example: "Now the idea of an omnipotent moral being, whose willing is a categorical imperative for all rational beings . . . is the idea of God" (22:127, Op. 207). Or again: "To prescribe all human duties as divine commands is already contained in every categorical imperative" (22:120, Op. 202). And if this suggests a conflation of the foundation of ethics with one of its objects—if not of ethics with religion—then a similar conflation between principles of ethics and principles of right seems to underlie passages such as the following: "The principle of right in the categorical imperative makes necessary the totality [*das All*] as absolute unity" (22:109.13–15; cf. 22:118, Op. 202). How are we to interpret passages like these? Kant himself gives us no help and provides no explanation of them in the *Opus postumum.* Once again, therefore, we need to take up these questions in his earlier writings in order to understand the position he arrives at in his last work.

In the *Critique of Pure Reason,* Kant's moral argument commences with a discussion of the idea of a moral world. A moral world is a possible world that would be realized by us if our freedom were in accordance with the moral law. We can think of such a world by abstracting from all hindrances to morality (such as inclinations). In such a world, Kant says, we would ourselves be the authors of both our own enduring happiness and that of others. For "freedom, partly inspired and partly restricted by moral laws" (A809), would itself be the cause of general happiness. In such a world, the harmony between morality and happiness has to be conceived "as necessary."[2]

In this context, 'happiness' clearly cannot be interpreted as the maximal satisfaction of sensuous desires or inclinations. It also does not consist simply in the consciousness of one's own virtue, as the Stoics maintained. Rather, Kant insists, the idea of a "self-rewarding morality" is correct only "on the condition that *everyone* does what he ought" (A810). What exactly Kant has in mind can be illustrated with the help of his *Reflexionen* from the late 1770s as well as his lectures on practical philosophy from the same time. In *Reflexion 6907*, for example, Kant notes: "There are two kinds of happiness: either it is itself the effect of the free will of rational beings, or it is a contingent happiness, depending externally on nature and being an effect thereof. By means of actions directed reciprocally at oneself and each other, rational beings can produce for each other true happiness which is independent from everything in nature. Without this, nature cannot yield proper happiness" (19:202). In other words, genuine moral happiness results from mutual virtue. It is independent of nature; that is why in the description of the moral world we can abstract from inclinations. There is in addition physical or empirical happiness qua satisfaction of our desires and inclinations. As a sensuous being I also seek empirical happiness, but this is dependent on nature and hence contingent. Moreover, without morality it is not genuine happiness at all.

The important point is that *we ourselves* could be the authors of such a moral world and, with it, of our mutual happiness. We do not have to presuppose God for its realization. Rather, in the *Critique of Pure Reason*, God enters the picture because not all people do what they ought to do from the moral point of view. Consequently, the individual's happiness is subject to chance and stands in a merely contingent relationship to her own virtue; she may as well abandon her hope for moral happiness. How about her empirical happiness? This, too, is by no means guaranteed, for all too often moral demands stand in conflict with a person's inclinations.

Yet the obligation or bindingness *(Verbindlichkeit)* of the moral law, the categorical 'You ought to', remains untouched thereby. Consequently, reason feels the need to assume a different connection between virtue and happiness than experience teaches (or, rather, does not teach), for it is "that same reason" after all that formulates the moral law, and yet also, under the name of "prudence" (A800, 806, 811, 813), has the unavoidable task of advancing my empirical happiness. Faced with an irreconcilable conflict between its two fundamental demands—happiness and morality—reason would have to despair, or at least turn away from the demands of morality. Being virtuous under such circumstances would be highly irrational. To account for the possibility of a non-empirical connection between happiness and morality is thus as essential to morality as the fundamental distinction between virtue and prudence. Thus Kant writes in the first *Critique:*

> Morality, by itself, constitutes a system. Happiness, however, does not do so, save in so far as it is distributed in exact proportion to morality. But this is possible only in the *intelligible* world, under a wise Author and Ruler. Such a Ruler, together with life in such a world, which we must regard as a future world, reason finds itself constrained to assume; otherwise it would have to regard the moral laws as empty figments of the brain, since without this presupposition the necessary consequence which it itself connects with these laws could not follow...Thus without a God and without a world invisible to us now but hoped for, the glorious ideas of morality are indeed objects of approval and admiration, but not *incentives* [*Triebfedern*] of purpose and action. For they do not fulfil in its completeness that end which is natural to every rational being and which is determined a priori, and

rendered necessary, by that same pure reason. (A811–813; my italics)

In his ethics lectures of the same years, Kant illustrates this point with the example of a universal peace. Such peace would be "correct in idea," as Kant puts it, and would be a state of universal justice (which it also presupposes), but as such it is merely *ideal,* for "the powers don't readily agree [*stimmen nicht sogleich überein*]" (27:137). Something similar is true of morality and happiness. In these lectures, too, Kant emphasizes that happiness would be "distributed widely" (27:138) if all human beings were to obey the moral law: indeed, in such case we could live even on an uninhabited island in the Arctic Ocean as if in paradise.[3] Not everyone, however, obeys the moral law. And the virtuous deeds of the individual are as insufficient for the realization of such paradise as are the just principles of an individual ruler for the realization of a universal peace. Without God the moral law would remain "correct in idea" and would, by presenting us with the idea of an unconditionally good action, permit a better distinction between different types of action (skillful, prudent, moral). Yet it would fail to propel us to act, since happiness would not accompany its realization: "No morality can . . . be practical without religion" (27:137).

Kant thus regards God's existence as a postulate, but as the condition of the possibility of the *obligatory force* of the moral law. If an existent is necessary as a condition for something that ought to happen, he writes in the *Critique,* then this something's existence is postulated: "Now since there are practical laws which are absolutely necessary, that is, the moral laws, it must follow that if these necessarily presuppose the existence of any being as the condition of the possibility of their *obligatory* power, this existence must be *postulated*" (A633f.). This being is God. "Thus God and a future life are two postulates which, according to the principles of pure reason, are inseparable from the obligation which that same reason imposes upon us" (A811).

The happiness that God distributes and that we may hope for if we are worthy of it is to be enjoyed in a "future world," in a "future life." For our happiness is precisely *not* determined by "the nature of the things of the world" (A810). Rather, as Kant elaborates in his lectures on ethics, the virtuous person hopes for happiness beyond "this miserable life . . . [and] in *analogy* with the physical world" (27:285; see *Lectures on Ethics*, 54). If this is so, however, then we are not thereby compelled to assume that God must also be "the author of nature." In order to distribute happiness in a future life or in an intelligible world, it does not follow that God needs to be credited with causal powers over *this* world.

Thus the argument of the *Critique of Pure Reason.* What may have motivated Kant to abandon it so quickly after its publication? And why did he become convinced, at about the same time, that the metaphysics of morals does require its own "critique" after all, or at least a *Groundwork*? For in 1781 a further critique that would precede the metaphysics of morals was nowhere envisioned (see A795–797).

The answer to these questions can, I believe, be found in the review of the *Critique of Pure Reason* by Christian Garve. I am not, however, thinking of the published version of the review that appeared anonymously in the *Göttingische Anzeigen von gelehrten Sachen* of January 19, 1782. This version had been rewritten by J. G. H. Feder and shortened by more than two thirds. More important is Garve's original version which he had sent to Kant on August 21, 1783, after reading in the *Prolegomena* that Kant challenged the reviewer to step out of his anonymity and engage in a fair debate (4:379–380).

In the present context I can leave aside Garve's treatment of the Transcendental Doctrine of Elements. More interesting is what he says about the Doctrine of Method, and especially about the concept of the highest good which I have just sketched. With regard to the latter, he writes: "It is very true that the moral feeling alone renders the thought of God significant for us . . . But that it is possible to retain this feeling and the truth founded on it after one has abandoned all remaining impressions relating to the existence of things, and the theory derived from them; that one can dwell and live in the realm of grace after the realm of nature has vanished before our eyes—this, I believe, will find its way into the hearts and minds of very few people."[4] Kant did not at all like what he read. In fact, as Hamann reported in a letter to Herder of December 1783, Kant felt he had been "treated like an *imbecille.*"[5] One month later, when Garve published his three-volume *Philosophische Anmerkungen und Abhandlungen zu Cicero's Büchern von den Pflichten,* accompanied by his own translation of Cicero's text, Kant seems to have made a beeline for it. For on February 18, Hamann could already write to J. G. Scheffner that Kant was now working on an Anti-Critique "against Garve's Cicero, as an indirect response to the latter's review [of his *Critique*]."[6] And in March, Hamann writes in the same vein: "The Anti-Critique will not address Garve's review directly, but more properly his 'Cicero,' and in this way will give him satisfaction for the former."[7] Kant, however, did not stick to this plan, for another month later Hamann had this to say: "Kant is now working on a *Prodromum* to his morals, which he initially wanted to call Anti-Critique, and which will deal with Garve's 'Cicero.'"[8] And then on May 2 he writes, again to Herder: "[Kant] is working hard on the completion of his system. The Anti-Critique of Garve's 'Cicero' has turned into a *Prodromum* of morals."[9] This "*Prodromum* of morals" is the *Groundwork to the Metaphysics of Morals,* which Kant completed in the fall of 1784 and which appeared at the Easter fair of the following year. By now Kant had decided to drop all explicit references to Garve. Hamann once again transmits the news to Herder;

this time his letter is dated March 28, 1785: "The *principium* of his [that is, Kant's] morals will appear at the next fair. The Appendix against Garve seems not to have materialized; rather, he is said to have shortened his work."[10] Be that as it may, Kant's quarrel with Garve's *Anmerkungen* to Cicero's book on duties can be witnessed on many pages of the *Groundwork,* if we read this text carefully and against the background of Garve's own position.[11]

At first glance, it must appear odd that Garve's comments on the Canon chapter of the first *Critique* should have had such an impact on Kant. In what Garve said about the Doctrine of Elements, for instance, Kant saw little more than grave misunderstandings of the doctrines he had expounded there. So let us look more closely at Garve's objections. There are three: (1) "That we recognize a certain conduct as absolutely worthy of happiness"; (2) "that this worthiness, more than happiness itself, is the final end of nature"; and (3) that, "after one has abandoned all remaining impressions relating to the existence of things, and the theory derived from them . . . reason gives us a priori to recognize certain necessary rules of conduct, which could not, however, be true, or at least could not be incentives for our will without God and a future life."

The last objection is no doubt the most important one. Although the first two objections also point to significant differences of opinion between Garve and Kant,[12] only the last one proceeds immanently and goes to the heart of Kant's argumentation. For Kant had claimed that I can hope to partake in happiness only if my reason imposes an order on my often conflicting inclinations and renders them coherent by subjecting them to a universal principle of action. Experience teaches us, however, that this, by itself, does not yield happiness—in fact, it often conflicts with happiness. Thus, if the principle of action is to determine my will to act morally, in spite of the fact that as a result my inclinations will temporarily go unsatisfied, I must be convinced of the retributive justice of a supreme author of the world. In the Dialectic of Pure Reason, however, Kant had just robbed his readers of their conviction that such a being exists. To this extent Garve is quite right, I think, when he insists that "very few people" will be able to understand how something that cannot be known by speculative reason is supposed to be of help to practical reason. Kant does point out that the moral law retains its obligatory force *(Verbindlichkeit)* for all actions even if no one acts in accordance with it. Moreover, he insists, it is precisely this moral *necessitation* which inevitably leads to the idea of God. But in this way he already presupposes the very bindingness which the idea of God was supposed to explain, and without whom the moral law was said to remain "an empty figment of the brain" and without any "incentive" for our actions.

It was through Garve's objection that Kant came to realize the *petitio principii* in his argument. For his notes on the published, abridged version of the review—in which these objections were dropped[13]—show clearly that be had not yet reached this realization. On the contrary, these notes indicate that Kant was working on his metaphysics of morals, which he hoped to publish "shortly," and which would not bother the reader "with idealism and categories."[14] Prior to receiving Garve's original review, then, Kant did not realize that the categorical imperative might indeed be an empty "figment of the brain" *(Hirngespinst)* (A811; see 4:445), and that consequently its reality must be demonstrated by a "critique of practical reason." Kant tried to provide such a demonstration in Chapter 3 of the *Groundwork.* It did, however, require recourse to "idealism and categories" and, moreover, presupposed the elimination of any divine incentives at the foundation of morality.

Kant's "Anti-Critique" of Garve's *Cicero* thus became the *Groundwork of the Metaphysic of Morals,* and the doctrine of our "worthiness to be happy" (first *Critique*) gave priority of place to a morality from "respect for the moral law" which requires no external "incentive" but follows directly from the autonomy of the subject. Yet Garve's influence is still clearly noticeable in the new theory of morality as respect for the moral law. "Respect for the law"—that means that I subordinate my will to a law of which I myself am the author. Consciousness of my duty and respect for the moral law are thus one and the same thing: "Duty is the necessity to act out of respect for the law," the *Groundwork* states (4:400); that something "is done for the sake of duty and so has a moral value" (4:406) are from now on synonymous expressions for Kant.

Interestingly, the moral concept of 'duty' did not occur even once in the *Critique of Pure Reason*.[15] It occurred, of course, all the more often in Garve's *Philosophische Anmerkungen und Abhandlungen zu Cicero's Büchern von den Pflichten*. But to Kant, Garve's philosophical analysis of this concept must have seemed completely inappropriate to the proper principle of morality—so inappropriate, indeed, that he now regarded it as absolutely necessary "to seek out and establish the supreme principle of morality" (4:392)—contrary to what he had asserted in the *Critique of Pure Reason*. For Garve had alleged (with Cicero) that all duties can be derived (with their *Verbindlichkeit*) from the four cardinal virtues of "prudence," "justice," "courage," and "temperance" (*Mäßigung*). These in turn are said to follow from our "human nature," that is, from our desire for knowledge, our sociability, our generosity (*Edelmut*), and our sense of order. The main motive for all our actions is our desire to satisfy our natural inclinations: "Whoever investigates the nature of what is good," Garve writes, "investigates the primary motives of our desires; and only from them can the grounds of morality be derived."[16]

In sharp opposition to Garve, Kant develops in Chapter 1 of his *Groundwork* a concept of duty which merely concerns the form of the will, that is, which requires no incentive for action other than the representation of the moral law itself. Consequently, the ultimate goal of our actions that is "inseparably" (A809) bound up with this law, the highest good, must be located not in an afterlife but in this life, in this world. This step in the argument is developed for the first time in Kant's essay "What Does It Mean to Orient Oneself in Thinking?" (1786), which is initiated by, and reflects his reception of, the so-called Pantheism debate *(Spinozastreit)* between Friedrich Jacobi and Moses Mendelssohn. It does not take much to see that Kant's classical doctrine of the postulates developed in his confrontation with this dispute. Commencing from Mendelssohn's repeated remark that, when confronted with Jacobi's claims about the role of "belief" in our knowledge of the world and ourselves, he feels the need to orient himself anew,[17] Kant provides some fundamental reflections on the concept of 'orientation', and on that of a 'need' of reason. Just as we cannot, for instance, orient ourselves in empirical space without a subjective ground of differentiation (that is, our bodily feeling of position), it is likewise impossible to orient ourselves in the supersensible realm without reason's subjective need to find an unconditioned for what is conditioned. Theoretical reason, however, knows only a hypothetical need of reason: if we *want* to form judgments about the first causes of what is contingent, we are then led to the assumption of an unconditioned being, as the *Critique of Pure Reason* had demonstrated. Yet such an employment of reason always remains contingent and regulative. Not so with practical reason: since we *must* judge with respect to what ought to be done, and hence cannot be oblivious regarding the possible success of what ought to be done, reason feels an unavoidable need to comprehend the possibility of its success.

With this we have reached a new, or second, stage of Kant's moral theology. The highest good is now the unconditioned corresponding to what is conditioned practically: the totality of the object of pure practical reason. Instead of the quest for the motivation or incentive for action, we face the question of the objective reality of such a concept. For a concept to have objective reality, the "real possibility" of its object must be demonstrable (see Bxxvi fn., A596fn.): in the case of the highest good, the real possibility of a proportional correspondence of virtue and happiness in this world needs to be demonstrated. Since the laws of nature do not imply such proportionality, yet the realization of the highest good in this world is unavoidably demanded by practical reason, a moral ruler of this world must be assumed who is capable of establishing the proportionality in question, and whose existence is therefore postulated: "For the pure practical employment of reason consists in the prescriptions of moral laws. They all lead, however, to the idea of the highest good that is possible *in this world,* insofar as it can be realized through freedom alone: morality. On the other side, they lead to what does not depend on human freedom alone, but also *on nature,* that is, the greatest happiness, insofar as it is distributed *in proportion* to the former" (8:139; my italics).

This position, presented here for the first time, is elaborated two years later in the *Critique of Practical Reason,* where the doctrine of the postulates of practical reason is presented in its classical form. Such a postulate of practical reason, Kant now writes, is a theoretical proposition that constitutes no object and hence founds no knowledge. Nevertheless, it expresses a subjective but true and unconditioned principle of reason "which is an inseparable corollary of an a priori unconditionally valid practical law" (5:122). It designates an existence as a condition necessary for the achievability (*Ausführbarkeit*) of moral actions: "practical reality" and "achievability" thus become equivalent terms for Kant (see 5:457). If I know that I can because I ought to, it must also be possible for me to know, if only in practical respect, that what is required by duty is possible.

Inevitably we notice that the concept of *happiness* in the highest good undergoes a corresponding shift. Since it is my duty to promote the highest good in this world, without being able to count on the virtue of others, my own happiness, which I can hope for to the extent that I am worthy of it, can no longer be interpreted as moral happiness, but only as physical, empirical happiness. In the *Critique of Practical Reason,* consequently, happiness is understood exclusively as empirical happiness. It now rests "on the harmony of *nature* with [my] entire end" (5:124). The fact that I as a physical being depend on sensuous objects and am at the mercy of nature is now the main obstacle to my own happiness, and no longer the fact that others do not do what they ought to do. Hence Kant withdraws the thesis of the first Critique that we could mutually be the authors of our own happiness. (Only now can the antinomy of practical reason arise!)[18]

Kant's new postulate for God's existence thus results from the fact that my empirical happiness is not within my own control because I do not have a thoroughgoing influence over the objects of my inclination. Even if I were completely virtuous, I would merely be capable of "an analogue of happiness" which Kant calls "self-contentment" (5:117). It expresses only the negative satisfaction with my own existence because I am conscious of being independent from inclinations in the determination of my will. The resulting unchanging contentment, Kant claims, since it rests on no particular feeling, can only be called intellectual contentment. To which we may add that in this respect it is akin to the aesthetic disinterestedness which is indifferent to the existence of the beautiful object. Inclinations, and hence happiness, do not know such disinterestedness; they are essentially tied to the existence of the objects of inclinations.

The necessity to postulate God's existence is thus a twofold one: on the one hand, this postulate must contain the sole possibility to think of nature in such a way that it does not frustrate the realization of my moral ends. On the other hand, it must contain the sole possibility to hope for an exact proportion, in this world, between virtue and happiness. To wit, the highest good is possible in the world "only on the supposition of a supreme cause of nature which has a causality corresponding to the moral disposition" (5:125). This argument still does not imply that God must also be the author of the world, but only that now and in the future he must be able to interact causally with it, and that he must know our moral dispositions. The God of the second *Critique* must be *summum bonum* and *summa intelligentia;* that he must also be *ens summum* does not yet follow from the moral argument.

It is just this amendment, among other things, that the *Critique of Judgment* provides by allowing us to interpret the highest good as the final end of creation (5:443). On the assumption of the autonomy of reflective judgment, we are entitled a priori to view nature itself as a purposive whole, and to relate the realization of the highest good to the plan underlying its creation. In this way there first arises the necessity to think the highest being not only as an intelligence and as legislating for nature, "but as a sovereign head legislating in the kingdom of ends," and to unite in the concept of God the traditional divine predicates (according to the categories): omniscient, omnipotent, all-just, and eternal/omnipresent. For this reason, Kant can now maintain: "In this way *moral* teleology supplements the deficiencies of *physical* teleology, and for the first time establishes a *theology*" (5:444).

With this we have reached what is widely regarded as the culmination, or the heart, of Kant's ethico-theology. At the same time it should have become apparent that Kant cannot rest content with this result, for the final end of creation cannot be the moral individuum and its individual happiness, but only mankind (humanity) as moral. So far, however, Kant had in his writings discussed the problem of morality solely from the point of view of the individual agent. Since not everyone does what she ought and what is required for the realization of a moral world or the highest good, Kant had concentrated on the question how the concept of happiness in proportion to moral worthiness can nevertheless acquire objective validity. The question of what needs to be done to bring about an ethical community had not yet come into view at all.[19]

This changes with Kant's *Religion within the Boundaries of Mere Reason.* Here we read for the first time of our duty to promote "the highest as a social [*gemeinschaftliches*] good" (6:97). For the realization of the highest good is impossible, Kant now argues, as long as man remains in the ethical state of nature, that is, in a state of moral corruption. Just as in the Hobbesian state of nature all men are in *status belli omnium in omnes* (as Kant corrects Hobbes 6:97), in the ethical state of nature all men are subject to continual attack on their virtuous disposition. Even the virtuous person is subject to such attack, no matter how much he himself esteems the moral law, simply because he is among men. With them, he is in a web of envy, greed, lust for power, and social rivalry, and consequently subject to a continuous temptation to violate the moral law: "It suffices that they are there, that they surround him, and that they are human beings, and they will mutually corrupt one another's moral disposition and make one another evil" (6:94).

According to Kant, mankind can rise above this ethical state of nature only if it succeeds in establishing a society in accordance with laws of virtue, that is, an ethical commonwealth or a moral people of God. This presupposes a politico-civil state for its realization, but it has a very different and unique "principle of unification" *(Vereinigungsprinzip),* namely, virtue, and hence a different form and constitution. Since the ethical commonwealth must be built upon laws of virtue, it is extended not just to a particular group of people but "ideally to the whole of mankind" (6:96); any actual political society can thus be regarded only as a "schema" of the ethical commonwealth.

Several comments are in order here. First, it is a moral duty to advance the highest good in the world. But because the highest good cannot be achieved merely by the moral efforts of the single individual but requires a union of such individuals into a whole toward the same goal, it follows that we also have a duty to leave the ethical state of nature and to form a "universal republic based on laws of virtue." It is indeed a duty of a special kind: one not of men toward men but "of the human race toward itself" (6:97). Yet, second, mankind is not in a position, Kant claims, to create an ethical commonwealth by itself. We can represent the form of such a commonwealth in its purity, but our sensuous nature is such that we cannot hope to make the highest good a reality without divine support: "To found a moral people of God is, therefore, a work whose execution cannot be hoped for from human beings but only from God himself" (6:100). (I will return to Kant's reasons for this claim shortly.) Third, the postulate for God's existence consequently requires another important emendation:

> Since by himself the human being cannot realize the idea of the highest good inseparably bound up with the pure moral disposition, either with respect to the happiness which is part of the good or with respect to the union of the human beings necessary to the fulfillment of the end, and yet there is also in him the duty to promote the idea, he finds himself driven to believe in the cooperation or the management of a moral ruler of the world, through which alone this end is possible. And here there opens up

before him the abyss of a mystery regarding what God may do, whether anything at all is to be attributed to him and what this something might be in particular, whereas the only thing that a human being learns from a duty is what he must himself do to become worthy of that fulfillment, of which he has no cognition or at least no possibility of comprehension. (6:139)

But now a new difficulty arises. We may think of a people of God under statutory laws, that is, a visible church united by a common belief in divine revelation. Yet this would not be the ethical commonwealth we have a duty to promote. An ethical union of mankind can only be one whose legislation is "purely internal" (6:100). Consequently, not only will its realization presuppose free, autonomous beings; but they must also reach inner "concord" *(Eintracht)"* and leave the ethical state of nature because of a changed *disposition* (6:95, 105).

I believe that Kant had in mind this veritable *"abyss* of a mystery" when in the *Opus postumum* he remarked repeatedly that not even God could make a morally good or morally bad person—one can only do it oneself. "That man acts morally can be *demanded* by God but not *made* or *coerced* by him" (21:57.8–9), Kant now wrote, for "it is not even in the divine power to make a morally good man (to make him morally good): He must do it himself" (21:83, Op. 249; see also 21:66.19–21). If this is so, however, the idea of a realization of the ethical commonwealth through God is not just incomprehensible but contradictory. At the same time, its realization remains a duty, since nowhere else but in the ethical commonwealth can the highest good become actual.

Doubts about the philosophical relevancy of such an alleged abyss of practical reason may have crossed Kant's mind as early as the Preface to the *Religion,* which was written only after all four parts of the text were completed. Thus he complemented his assertion that morality extends itself to the idea of a powerful moral lawgiver *outside* of mankind with the question, But how is such a proposition a priori possible? To which he himself replied: "The key to the solution of this problem, *so far as I believe myself to understand it,* I can only indicate here and not develop" (6:6fn.; my italics). This footnote does not explicitly mention the ethical commonwealth, but it does mention what Kant at the time regarded as the main reason why such a commonwealth cannot come about without God's intervention: the "natural characteristic of man" that for all of his actions he must conceive of an end over and above the law.[20] And Kant concludes with the conditional: "But now, if the strictest obedience to the moral laws is to be thought of as the cause of the ushering in of the highest good (as end), then, since human capacity does not suffice to effect happiness in the world proportionate to the worthiness to be happy, an omnipotent moral being must be assumed as ruler of the world, under whose care this would come about, i.e., morality leads inevitably to religion" (6:7–8fn.).

Does this conditional amount to a revocation of what Kant previously had thought demonstrable? At the very least, it appears that alternative ways of considering the relationship between morality and happiness are no longer excluded categorically. And the fact remains that, in the course of surveying Kant's ethico-theology, we have been presented with at least four different arguments as to why it is necessary to postulate God's existence—a fact that, at the very least, puts into question the alleged necessity for acting ("achievability") that is required of a practical postulate of something as existing. These four versions of the postulate were:

1. God as incentive;
2. God as distributor of individual happiness in proportion to virtue;

3. God as guarantor of the harmony of nature with the moral law;

4. God as founder of the ethical commonwealth.

We have already seen that Kant withdrew the first postulate as early as 1785. And fundamental doubts arise just now with regard to the fourth one. The third postulate is undermined by the doctrine of theoretical self-positing. For if Kant is right in claiming that the moving forces of matter "are what the moving subject itself does with its body to other bodies," then, from the standpoint of self-positing, the harmony of nature and human purposiveness is guaranteed by the actuality of our experience. Consequently, it is not necessary to postulate God's existence in order to be able to think of nature in such a way "that in the conformity to law of its form it at least harmonizes with the ends to be effected in it according to the laws of freedom" (5:176).

This leaves us with the postulate of God as the "distributor" (5:128) of happiness in proportion to our worthiness to be happy. Yet the practical necessity or inevitability of this postulate must also become doubtful when we note that, in the *Religion*, Kant identifies the highest good as the final end of creation with the ethical commonwealth as a system of well-disposed people, or the moral world.[21] Not surprisingly, he now returns to the *moral* concept of happiness that is once again contrasted explicitly with a merely physical happiness ("freedom from evils and enjoyment of ever-increasing pleasures" [6:67]). This "moral happiness" consists, rather, in the consciousness of "the reality and *constancy* of a disposition that always advances in goodness" (6:67; see also 6:75). As such, it is in principle accessible and within the reach of the human agent.

Interestingly, in the Preface to the *Religion*, Kant opposes to the synthetic judgment that asserts the existence of God "outside of mankind" another sentence that he characterizes as analytic. He describes it thus: "Agreement with the mere idea of a moral lawgiver for all human beings is indeed identical with the moral concept of duty in general, and to this extent the proposition *commanding the agreement* would be analytic" (6:6; my italics). With this Kant reconnects with an argument that was first stated in Book 3 of the *Religion* (see 6:98–100), and that introduced a new idea of God, moreover, one that is entirely independent of the doctrine of the postulates. (We might call this the fourth stage of Kant's ethicotheology.) It can briefly be summarized as follows.

An ethical commonwealth is a union of all people under public laws. Since the legislation is to be an ethical one—what matters is not the legality of actions, as in a juridical commonwealth, but the disposition or *Gesinnungen* from which the actions spring—the people as a people, or its common will, cannot itself be the lawgiver. Unlike the legality of actions, which meets public criteria, dispositions are inner states and not accessible to others—sometimes not even to the agent herself (see 4:407). We cannot judge others morally. Hence someone other than the populace must be the public lawgiver for an ethical commonwealth. At the same time, the laws must not be thought of as statutory laws emerging originally from the will of this other, or else they would not be ethical laws, and the corresponding duties would not be free duties of virtue. "Therefore," Kant concludes,

> only such a one can be thought of as the supreme lawgiver of an ethical commonwealth with respect to whom all *true duties*, hence also the ethical, must be represented as *at the same time* his commands; consequently, he must also be "one who knows the heart," in order to penetrate to the most intimate parts of the disposition of each and everyone and, as must be in every commonwealth, give to each according to the worth of his actions. But this is

> the concept of God as moral ruler of the world.
> Hence an ethical commonwealth is conceivable
> only as a people under divine commands, i.e., as a
> *people of God,* and indeed *in accordance with the
> laws of virtue.* (6:99)

This concept of God is independent of the doctrine of postulates. It is connected analytically with the concept of duty, or better, with the categorical imperative insofar as the latter is thought as the "principle of unification" *(Vereinigungsprinzip)* of free moral beings. As such, Kant emphasizes, God has to be thought in a threefold quality, namely, as omnipotent and holy legislator, as benevolent ruler and preserver of the human race, and as administrator of his own holy laws, that is, as righteous judge. The idea of such a moral ruler of the world, in whom legislature, executive, and jurisdiction are united, lies "in the concept of a people regarded as a commonwealth, where such a threefold superior power *(pouvoir)* is always to be thought, except that the people is here represented as ethical, and hence the threefold quality of the moral sovereign of the human race, which in a juridico-civil state must of necessity be distributed among three different subjects, can be thought as united in one and the same being." And the belief in such a being, Kant adds explicitly, "really contains no mystery, since it expresses solely God's moral bearing toward the human race. It also presents itself spontaneously to human reason everywhere and is therefore to be met with in the religion of most civilized peoples" (6:140). With these remarks I can finally turn to Kant's *Opus postumum.*

Kant returns to the problem of God's existence toward the end of the *Opus postumum.* This takes place on sheets 9, 10, and 5 of the fifth fascicle and in the first fascicle—hence immediately following the *Selbstsetzungslehre*. Empirical self-consciousness, he had argued in the preceding pages, can emerge only in the context of a single, all-embracing whole of moving forces, in the progressive determination of which I posit myself as a physical object in space and time. But—and this is the new and important thought in the sheets to be considered now—I do not only posit myself as an object. I also constitute myself as a person, that is, as a being whose actions can be imputed to me. And this, Kant seems to claim, also presupposes a collective unity of forces, albeit not of matter, but forces of moral-practical reason.

How is this to be understood? Let me first cite the passage which marks Kant's transition from theoretical to practical self-positing:

> There is an all-comprehending nature (in space and time) in which reason coordinates all physical relations into unity. There is a universally ruling operative cause with freedom in rational beings, and, [given] with the latter, a categorical imperative which connects them all, and, with that, in turn, an all-embracing, morally commanding, original being—a God. The phenomena from the moving forces of moral-practical reason, in so far as they are a priori with respect to men in relation to one another, are the ideas of right...There is a God: for there is in moral-practical reason a categorical imperative, which extends to all rational world-beings and through which all world-beings *are united.* (22:104–105, Op. 198; my italics)

As a first approximation, I propose the following elaboration. Reason comes into being (generally speaking) when the original spontaneity of the power of representation limits itself or imposes laws upon itself. In order to posit oneself, the task is consequently to anticipate "possible forces affecting reason" (21:83, Op. 249) in the apprehension of which such self-limitation can occur. This holds for practical as well as theoretical reason. Just as I appear to myself as corporeal to the extent that I am conscious of being affected, I appear to myself as free in a practical sense to the extent that I overcome the immediate impressions on my faculty of desire and determine myself to action, "by calling up representations of what, in a more indirect manner, is useful or injurious" (A802). In this way I recognize through experience my own practical freedom as one of nature's causes, namely, as a causality of reason in the determination of my will (see A803).

"By 'the practical' I mean everything that is possible through freedom," Kant wrote at A800, thus also making clear that not everything is possible through freedom. At the level of *Willkür*, my will is constrained by various empirical conditions that, when made explicit, enter into the formulations of rules of skill and counsels of prudence. But my freedom is also constrained by the fact that it coexists with other free rational beings like myself. The limiting condition of my own freedom is the freedom of every other. The laws operative at this level must emerge from freedom itself, for freedom can be constrained and remain free only if it itself has authored the laws it subjects itself to. At the moment when freedom imposes its own law upon itself, in the form of the categorical imperative, the concepts of duty and right arise as a consequence thereof, and it is in this context that, according to Kant, I posit myself as a person. 'Person' is here defined as a being that not only thinks but also can say to itself 'I think' (21:103.19–20); a being, in other words, that can distance itself from the world of sense and, because also endowed with a will, can command its own nature, and yet, in virtue of the numerical identity of the 'I,' remain the same imputable subject throughout. A person, for this reason, is "a being capable of rights, who can encounter wrong or can consciously do it, and who stands under the categorical imperative" (22:55, Op. 214). In this sense, then, Kant can speak in the passage cited above of the categorical imperative as a principle that "connects" or "unites" all rational world-beings endowed with a will. But why should this also imply the proposition 'There is a God'?

Most violations of our imperatives of skill and prudence nature rebuffs with failure: the chosen means do not yield the desired end. Not so with violations of the law of morality: here nature remains mute. A practical law, however, even one that I give to myself, can be regarded as a *law* only if its transgressions may be accompanied by sanctions in accordance with principles. A law to which no consequences were attached, or, even worse, whose violation I could forgive myself, would be null and void as a law (cf. 6:438–439). Hence it must follow from the mere but completely determined concept of a universally valid moral law: "There must also, however, be—or at least be thought—a legislative force *(potestas legislatoria)* which gives these laws emphasis (effect) although only in idea" (22:126, Op. 207).

Thus it becomes clear that it is the analytically derived concept of God from Book 3 of the *Religion,* as the moral sovereign of the ethical commonwealth, that is operative in these fascicles of the *Opus postumum.* It is not the hope for happiness attainable only through God's intervention that here leads to the assumption of a highest moral being, but the reflection on the implications of the concept of a moral law as the human "principle of unification" in conjunction with practical self-positing. This need not mean that happiness plays no role whatsoever in ethics anymore. But Kant now builds on the realization that the highest good as the inseparable goal of moral reason can only be a social one, a common world based on laws of virtue. The duty I have to promote this commonwealth equals the duty to regard the categorical imperative as a "principle of unification" of all rational beings in it. And the concept of an ethical commonwealth, in turn, entails the concept of a moral ruler of the world in whom legislature, executive, and jurisdiction are united, as the *Religion* had argued. "*Every human being* is, in virtue of *his freedom* and of the law which *restricts* it, made subject to necessitation through his moral-practical reason, [and] stands under command and prohibition ... A command, to which everyone must absolutely give obedience, is to be regarded by everyone as from a being which rules and governs over all. Such a being, as moral, however, is called God. So there is a God" (22:120–127, Op. 203–7).[22]

Kant is now eager to emphasize, however, that this does not imply God's existence as a substance outside my thinking. What is crucial to him is the fact that I could not posit myself *as a person* unless I placed myself in a context of right and duty that unifies all rational world-beings, a context that itself depends on God for its possibility. The concept or ideal of God is thus as essential for practical *Selbstsetzung* as the concept of the ether was for theoretical *Selbstsetzung*. Indeed, it is noteworthy how parallel the two acts of self-positing are for Kant. To some extent, such parallel treatment was already anticipated in those earlier writings that characterized the right as an equality of action and reaction according to the law of freedom (see 5:464–465, 6:232, 8:292). At the same time, the *Opus postumum* now shows signs of terminological ambiguity or uncertainty that suggest that a position is undergoing significant revisions. In the present context, this is of interest especially with the case of Kant's concept of a postulate.

For both theoretical and practical reason, Kant lists axioms. That of theoretical reason is: "There is [only] one space and one time" (22:101.18–19; see also 22:610, Op. 98). The axiom of practical reason is: "There is [only] one God" (22:108.14), or only one (ethical) right. Since God is the sovereign of the moral world, he can only be one, as there can be only one being who has only rights and no duties.

Theoretical reason also has a postulate: "In virtue of its moving forces, a body is immediately present to other bodies or any other matter at a distance (i.e. through empty space) through Newtonian attraction" (22:113.25–27). Does practical reason have a postulate? This would be the proposition 'God exists'. But as soon as Kant puts forward this postulate, he provides it with an important qualification: "The existence of such a being, however, can only be *postulated* in a practical respect: Namely, the necessity of acting in such a way as if I stood under such a fearsome—but yet, at the same time, salutary—guidance and also guarantee, in the knowledge of all my duties as divine commands *(tanquam non ceu);* hence the *existence* of such a being is not postulated in this formula, which would be self-contradictory" (22:116, Op. 200).

What is postulated in the sentence 'God exists', then, is not properly the existence of a being independent of human thought and action (this would be "self-contradictory" since God is *analytically* connected with the concept of duty). Rather, what is thus postulated is what endows practical reason's ideas of right with "moving force" and makes possible their unity: "The a priori relation of right as *moral compulsion*" (22:129, Op. 208; my italics). To this end they must be viewed as emerging from a moral sovereign of the human race, although it is practical reason itself from which moral compulsion springs. 'God exists' means, therefore, that he exists in practical reason; *"est Deus in nobis"* (22:130, Op. 209), Kant records with Ovid, and explicates a little later: "It cannot be denied that such a being exists; yet it cannot be asserted that it exists outside rationally thinking man" (22:55, Op. 214).

This sheds new light on the often repeated phrase of our "human duties *as* divine commands." Unlike Kierkegaard, Kant insists that a divine command issued directly to us could not be regarded as just that: the modal 'as' becomes for him an 'as if', an *instar* or *tamquam* (see, e.g., 21:28, Op. 232) that requires no external legislator: "There can be no doubt that no command or prohibition can really have been issued to man by a holy, powerful being, or, if this were to have happened, that man could not have perceived this voice and convinced himself of its reality. Thus there is *no alternative* but to regard the knowledge of our duties as *instar* divine commands, which do not lose any of their authority because of the inevitable ignorance of such prophecy. Therefore, the moral imperative can be regarded as the voice of God" (22:64.21–29; first italics mine; cf. 7:63).

We can now describe Kant's position more clearly. Reason constitutes itself through the formulation of two ideals with their respective conditions of unity, in relation to which the open-ended self-determination of the subject can proceed. For theoretical reason, the question is: "How are laws for the united space- and time-determinations of moving forces possible a priori? Newton's work. Immediate *actio in distans* (through empty space)" (22:56, Op. 214). For practical reason, the question is: How is the unity of the moral world possible? To this end it provides for itself the ideal of God as "a highest being who puts all rational world-beings in the unity of moral relationships" (22:113.18–19). This ideal of God, however, is nothing other than "pure practical reason in its personality, *with reason's moving forces in respect to world-beings and their forces*" (22:118, Op. 202; my italics).

There is universal attraction (Kant says as a Newtonian) only if there is matter in space. If space were empty, there would be no attraction, but also no experience. Once we assume a body in space, we also have to think the forces that it exerts. These are, of course, only appearances. That is, in the *Opus postumum* no less so than in the first *Critique*, space, and with it the forces in it, are to be understood as transcendentally *ideal*: "The thinking subject also creates for itself a world, as object of possible experience in space and time. This object is only one world. Moving forces are inserted in the latter (e.g. attraction and repulsion) without which there would be no perceptions; but only what is formal" (21:23, Op. 227). Correspondingly, we would have to say that there is a God only if there are finite rational beings endowed with a will. As soon as we assume such beings, we also have to think of the moral law of reason, of the categorical imperative as the principle of their unity in an ethical commonwealth, and hence of a moral sovereign of such beings: "Reason inevitably creates objects for itself. Hence everything that thinks has a God" (21:83, Op. 248). And into this representation of God, one might add, we "insert" those moving forces, without which there would be no common morality. "Newtonian attraction through empty space and the freedom of man are analogous concepts to each other: They are categorical imperatives—*ideas*" (21:35, Op. 237).

One problem remains, however. If God is an ideal of pure practical reason, we must think of him (in the moral sense) as all-powerful moral sovereign. We must therefore also assume a world, in order to give meaning to the idea of God as a practical being. Practical reason is compelled to assume a "real opposition" between God and world, if the moral idea of God is to have practical reality. "The division into God and the world is not analytic (logical) but synthetic: that is, through real opposition ... How, then, does their combination acquire reality?" (21:22, Op. 229, 228). How are we to understand the thought that God is active in this world, that he has power over nature? In the *Religion,* Kant had written with regard to God's contribution to the realization of the highest good in the world that there opens up before us "the abyss of a mystery" regarding what God may do in this respect. In the *Opus postumum,* he has gone a step further.

On the one hand, we cannot comprehend a free interference by an extraworldly substance with the law-governed course of nature: "No miracles take place in the corporeal world," Kant pronounced in an earlier passage of the *Opus postumum*, and also in the so-called "Kiesewetter Aufsätze" (21:439.18; 18:320–22). On the other hand, God cannot realize what is morally good directly through men. God can *demand* that we act morally but *cannot make* us do so. "The question whether God could not give man a better will would amount to this: that he should make it the case that [man] wills what he does not will." And "It is not even in the divine power to make a morally good man (to make him morally good): He must do it himself" (21:37, 83, Op. 239, 249). Thus the ideas of God and the world are entirely "heterogeneous" (21:22, Op. 228). If the concept of God is to have practical reality, and if transcendental philosophy is to be systematic, both ideas have to be thought of as standing in "real relations." Consequently, a third idea is required, in the light of which the ideas of God and world are united in one system. This, according to Kant, can be none other than that of "man in the world, restricting himself through laws of duty" (21:59, Op. 244)—of a being of nature that is at the same time subject to the categorical imperative. This (as Kant puts it) "*ideal*, the archetype *(prototypon)*, of a man adequate to duty" (21:40, Op. 240) is *the wise man*, whose use of reason, be it theoretical or practical, is entirely appropriate to every situation. It is the ideal of the true philosopher, the *philos* of *sophia*, an ideal we never reach in our lifetime but which practical reason nevertheless sets us as a task. Not surprisingly, the concept of a highest good, so central to Kant's earlier writings on ethics and religion, is now mentioned only in passing: it is no longer the concept of a world, but a concept of the subject.[23] It signifies "wisdom" or the "complete unity" (21:22, Op. 229) of theoretical and practical reason: "There is here then a relation of two heterogeneous objects, a relation of efficient causes *(nexus causalis)*, indeed; if the *totality* of beings is thought, however, then this is subjective rather than objective (lying not in the things but in the thinking subject): the highest good (the original and the derivative)" (21:22, Op. 228). Kant thus reappropriates the Greek concept of the highest good as a state of the subject from which, several decades earlier, his reflections on this topic had commenced.[24]

With this account Kant has finally also solved one of the oldest problems in his philosophy: the problem of the unity of theoretical and practical reason. This solution comprises both the *origin* of the dual use of reason in man's self-positing spontaneity, and the reconcilability of their respective *objects* (God and world) in man as a natural being, restricted by laws of duty. "God, the world, and what unites both into a system: the thinking, innate principle of man in the world *(mens)*" (21:34, Op. 237). Moral law and the law of nature are thus "ultimately [combined] in one single philosophical system," as the *Critique of Pure Reason* had demanded (A840): in the system of transcendental philosophy as *Selbstsetzungslehre*. With this Kant has reached a position which he himself describes as "the highest standpoint of transcendental philosophy." Transcendental philosophy, in Kant's final synthesis, is the systematic unity of three ideas that are jointly necessary for the self-constitution of reason, or for the subject's theoretical and practical *Selbstsetzung:* "Transcendental philosophy," Kant now writes, "is the act of consciousness whereby the subject becomes the originator of itself and, thereby, also of the whole object of technical-practical and moral-practical reason in one system" (21:78, Op. 245).

In this final system of transcendental philosophy, in which theoretical and practical reason are united at last, practical reason shares the philosophical agnosticism to which theoretical reason found itself obligated as early as 1781. Whether God exists outside our thoughts cannot be decided philosophically, neither theoretically nor practically. What is more, in transcendental philosophy, Kant now insists, we cannot even ask this question (see 22:52–53, Op. 212). In this discipline, reason only examines its own principles—principles through which it constitutes itself as both theoretical and practical reason. Whereas the *Religion* had still maintained that morality leads ineluctably to religion, through which it extends itself to the postulate of a divine being *outside* of mankind, in the *Opus postumum* Kant endorses only the first part of this claim, and with an important qualification. Of religion he now asserts that it does *not* consist in the belief in a substance (see also 21:143) and explains: "Religion is conscientiousness *(mihi hoc religioni).* The holiness of the acceptance [*Zusage*] and the truthfulness of what man must confess to himself. Confess to yourself. To have religion, the concept of God is not required (still less the postulate: 'There is a God')" (21:81, Op. 248).

In the end, then, ethics and religion coincide. In the *Opus postumum,* the classical doctrine of the postulates of pure practical reason is finally laid to rest.

CHAPTER SIX

"I Regard Reason as the Beginning of the Understanding"

In this last chapter I take the liberty of stepping back, to some extent at least, from Kant's text to view his final synthesis in comparison with two other thinkers, one from his own time, one from ours. In this way, I hope an interesting aspect of the *Opus postumum* will come into clearer focus than might otherwise be the case.

"I regard reason as the beginning of the understanding." Thus Hölderlin wrote to Friedrich Schiller in a letter of August 1797, sixteen years after the publication of Kant's *Critique of Pure Reason.* I want to use this statement as an opportunity to reflect on a phenomenon that must initially puzzle every reader of the *Opus postumum,* namely, the apparent reversal of the relation of dependence between reason and understanding that Kant gave in the *Critique.* For in the first *Critique,* it is not reason that is the beginning of the understanding but the reverse: "All our knowledge starts with the senses, proceeds from thence to understanding, and ends with reason," he wrote unambiguously (A298). And "Understanding may be regarded as a faculty which secures the unity

[148]

of appearances by means of rules, and reason as being the faculty which secures the unity of the rules of understanding under principles. Accordingly, reason never applies itself directly to experience or to any object, but to understanding, in order to give to the manifold knowledge of the latter an a priori unity by means of concepts" (A302).

The concepts through which reason produces its unity are the ideas. Kant characterizes them in a way that likewise leaves no doubt that he regards the understanding as prior to reason—for reason, he declares, depends for its own concepts on the categories of the understanding: "In the first place we must recognize that pure and transcendental concepts can issue only from the understanding. Reason does not really generate any concept. The most it can do is to *free* a concept of *understanding* from the unavoidable limitations of possible experience, and so to endeavour to extend it beyond the limits of the empirical, though still, indeed, in terms of its relation to the empirical" (A408f.). It is Kant's view that, just as the categories derive from the forms of judgment when applied to an object of intuition in general, the ideas of reason spring from the form of syllogisms when applied to the unity of intuition under the direction of the categories. More precisely, they are concepts of the totality of the conditions for any given conditioned (see A321f.). Ideas of reason are thus properly speaking nothing but "categories [of relation] extended to the unconditioned" (A409).

According to the first *Critique*, then, the understanding is the beginning of reason. And it is precisely this relationship that Hölderlin wishes to reverse. For him, "the idea is prior to the concept," as he writes in the letter to Schiller, "just as the tendency is prior to the (determined, rule-governed) deed" (StA 6:249). I will set aside for now the question whether he means the same by these expressions as does Kant. What is intriguing is the fact that Kant himself, toward the end of his philosophical career, felt compelled to reverse the order of reason and understanding. About this there cannot be any doubt, either: "Reason precedes, with the projection of its forms," Kant wrote in the last fascicle of the *Opus postumum* (21:15, Op. 222). And in another passage, he states explicitly of the faculty of reason: "This is not the logical employment of reason, which merely concerns the formal element of knowledge, but is originator of itself" (21:106.18–20). Of the ideas of reason Kant now writes: "*Ideas* precede appearances in space and time" (21:88, Op. 252). These are no longer the ideas of the first *Critique,* no longer concepts of the understanding freed of the limitations of possible experience, but rather are representations generated by reason itself: "Ideas are images [*Bilder*] (intuitions), created a priori through pure reason, which, [as] merely subjective thought-objects and elements of knowledge, precede knowledge of things" (21:51, Op. 242). This is clearly no longer the doctrine of the first *Critique.* How is this to be understood?

I begin with Hölderlin. It may seem natural to assume that Hölderlin's reversal of the relation between understanding and reason is due to Jacobi's influence on him. For Jacobi had insisted, in opposition to Kant's first *Critique,* that an inevitable and unavoidable feeling, an "immediate consciousness of a spirit and God [*unmittelbares Geistes- und Gottesbewußtsein*]," lies at the bottom of all philosophizing—a feeling that Jacobi himself later called "reason" in order "to distinguish it from the senses for the perceptible world."[1] And Jacobi's influence on Hölderlin is by now well documented.[2] In the letter I have quoted, however, Hölderlin even seems to go beyond Jacobi. He states explicitly that not only "essentially" but also "actually with regard to time, in the historical development of human nature, the idea is prior to the concept, just as the tendency is prior to the (determined, rule-governed) deed. I regard reason as the beginning of the understanding." If we read these sentences against the background of Hölderlin's novel *Hyperion,* whose first volume had been published in the same year and which Hölderlin had sent to Schiller with his previous letter, it becomes clear that Hölderlin is here playing with a thought not of Jacobi's but of Hamann's. I am thinking of Hamann's astonishing thought that, just as painting preceded writing, song preceded declamation, and barter preceded trade, in the same way poetry—poetic reason—preceded colloquial language, so that poetry is the mother tongue of the human race, or, as the so-called "Oldest System Program of German Idealism" calls it, "the teacher [*Lehrmeisterin*] of humanity."[3]

When Hölderlin sends a dedication copy of his *Hyperion* to the Princess Auguste von Homburg, he returns to this theme in his inscription for the princess: "Poets generally emerge at the beginning or end of a world epoch. With song the peoples descend from the heaven of their childhood into the life of activity, into the land of culture [*Kultur*]. With song they return again to primordial life. Art is the bridge from nature to culture [*Bildung*], and from culture to nature. The author" (StA 3, 575).

The poetic word, the song, thus precedes any determinate action that is directed toward an object distinct from the agent. Poesy makes originally possible the transition from nature to conscious activity. Poesy is meant here in the original sense of the word, in the sense of ποιειν, of "making," of "creating," or "bringing about." What is created in the poetic word is a way of world encounter, the opening of a space, of an original distance in which things can appear and be brought under control by naming them. According to Hölderlin, in the beginning—in the prepoetic state of nature—man does not know "that there is something else out-side of himself." In the beginning, he lets Hyperion say, "man and his gods were one, when unknown to itself, eternal beauty *was*" (H 64f.; StA 3:79). It is man's inner fullness, his abundance, that eventually compels him to go outside himself and that demands exhibition. "The first child of human, of divine Beauty is art," we read in *Hyperion*. "He wants to feel himself, therefore he sets his Beauty over against himself. Thus did man give himself his gods" (H 65; StA 3:79). It is from such poetic articulation of an eternal, divine state of being that Hyperion lets philosophy emerge. Poetry is the beginning (as well as the end) of philosophy, he says. The lat-ter springs from the former like Minerva from the head of Jupiter. The very being of Beauty, which at first is only felt and set over against oneself in the world of gods, can now be grasped, named, and comprehended:

> The great saying, the εν διαφερον εαυτω (the one differentiated in itself) of Heraclitus, could be found only by a Greek, for it is the very being of Beauty, and before that was found there was no philosophy ... The moment of beauty was now well known to men, it was there in life and thought, the infinitely one existed. It could be ana-lyzed, taken apart in men's minds, it could be re-constituted from its components, and so the being of the highest and the best could be increasingly known, and the knowledge of it be set up as the law in all the multifarious realms of the spirit. (H 67; StA 3:81f.)

The knowledge of the highest and best be set up as the law in all the multifarious realms of the spirit: Hölderlin tried to convert this rather poetic image of the understanding's ground in *Hyperion* into a philosophical "sketch" in a letter to his brother of June 2, 1796. There he described the relation of reason and understanding in the following way.

Reason lays the ground, the understanding comprehends. More precisely, reason lays the ground with its principles (*Grundsätze*), which are laws of thought and action that are related to what Hölderlin views as the universal conflict in man. This universal conflict is the conflict between the striving toward the absolute on the one hand, and the striving for limitation on the other. It is a conflict that characterizes the human situation in what he calls the *Urtheilung*, or "original separation."[4] The primordial being of which Hyperion speaks passed into the *Urtheilung* when we became conscious. As an original unity of subject and object that precedes every relation of a subject to an object, this "being" can never itself become an object of knowledge. Nevertheless, it is anticipated in all our actions as an ideal which we long to restore and toward which our conscious life is oriented. Reason refers its principles to this ideal being as the highest ground of all, and thus "grounds" its principles. They demand in specific ways that the conflict between the opposing strivings be remedied. If the principles are applied to such conflict and yield a general reconciliation, they result in universal concepts of the understanding, "e.g., the concepts of substance and accidence, of action and reaction, of duty and right, etc. These concepts are for the understanding what the ideal is for reason. Just as reason forms its laws in accordance with the ideal, the understanding forms its maxims in accordance with these concepts" (StA 6:209).

It is noteworthy that for Hölderlin the understanding regulates both the theoretical and the practical domains. The concepts of right and duty belong to the understanding's provenance just as do those of action and reaction, or of substance and accidence. Reason, by contrast, provides the supreme division into the theoretical and the practical by generating laws of thought and action that relate the conflicting tendencies in man to the ideal of beauty. This reason is not, however, the "mere" reason *(die bloße Vernunft)*, the "king of the North," as Hyperion calls the Kantian theory disparagingly, but the "striving" reason whose sole and unifying ideal is that of beauty. Kant's doctrine does not come off well here at all. Hyperion describes it in the following way. The understanding is like a journeyman who constructs a fence as it has been sketched out for him for the garden that his master intends to plant: "The understanding's entire business is makeshift." Reason is like an overseer whom the master of the house has set over the servants; but "he knows as little as they do what will come of their endless toil." Mere reason, Hyperion insists, produces no philosophy, just as little as mere understanding, "for philosophy is more than the blind demand for ever greater progress in the combination and differentiation of some particular material. But once the divine $\epsilon\nu$ $\delta\iota\alpha\phi\epsilon\rho o\nu$ $\epsilon\alpha\upsilon\tau\omega$, which is striving reason's ideal of Beauty, shines out, it does not demand blindly; it knows why and to what end it demands" (H 68; StA 3:83).

If we read this as a critique of Kant, I think it falls short on at least two counts. First, already in the *Critique* of 1781 Kant refers reason to an ultimate end, namely, the highest good, or to wisdom. Even in the first *Critique* reason is consequently more than a "blind demand for ever greater progress in the combination and differentiation of some particular material" (see A850). Second, moreover, in the *Groundwork to the Metaphysics of Morals* of 1785, Kant gives a characterization of reason that differs significantly from that of the first *Critique*:

> Now man actually finds in himself a power which distinguishes him from all other things—and even from himself so far as he is affected by objects. This power is *reason.* As pure spontaneity reason is elevated even above *understanding* in the following

respect. Understanding—although it too is spontaneous activity and is not, like sense, confined to
ideas which arise only when we are affected by
things (and therefore are passive)—understanding
cannot produce by its own activity any concepts
other than those whose sole service is *to bring sensuous ideas under rules* and so to unite them in one
consciousness: without this employment of sensibility it would think nothing at all. Reason, on the
other hand—in what are called 'Ideas'—shows a
spontaneity so pure that it goes far beyond anything sensibility can offer: it manifests its highest
function in distinguishing the sensible and intelligible worlds from one another and so in marking out
limits for understanding itself. (4:452)

This passage obviously implies an extension of the concept of
reason found in the first *Critique*. It does not yet seem to
imply a reversal of the relation of understanding and reason—unless, that is, one wanted to bring into play here the
primacy of what is practical on which Kant always insists.
But that would be misguided. After all, the *Critique of Pure
Reason* first had to demonstrate that a practical employment
of reason was not impossible; as Kant put it six years later, it
had to deny knowledge in order to make room for faith
(Glaube) (Bxxx).[5] Be that as it may, what Kant has to say in
the *Opus postumum* about the relation of reason and understanding is motivated by different considerations. It is to
these that I want to turn next.

First, however, we must discern Kant's motive for the cor-
relation of understanding and reason in the *Critique*.[6] In the
course of the history of Western philosophy, both terms repeatedly reversed their roles and referents,[7] and Kant, in his
pre-critical writings, never distinguished systematically between them. Thus he still used "understanding" *(intelligen-*

tia) and "reason" *(rationalitas)* indiscriminately in the In-
augural Dissertation of 1770.[8] But this was bound to change
with the discovery of the antinomies of reason. With their
discovery came the realization that reason must be prepared
not only for errors in its judgments but also for "contradictions within its own laws" (28:620) that generate illusions as
soon as reason attempts to determine the unconditioned. The
antinomies thus force pure reason to set limits to its own theoretical employment, and to be guided by the distinction between appearances and things in themselves. Since this in
turn is the sole condition for the possibility of genuine
morality, Kant can later boast, in the *Critique of Practical
Reason,* that the antinomies of pure reason were the most
fortunate perplexities in which human reason could ever have
become involved (5:107).

But the *Critique of Pure Reason* itself can only lay claim to
a "negative use" as its greatest achievement, namely, that of
"guarding against error" (A795). To this end, however, Kant
had to demonstrate how reason derives its ideas from the categories, and how fallacies arise unavoidably when they are
used not regulatively in the systematization of the knowledge
obtained by the understanding, but constitutively and yet independently of the conditions of sensibility. "The dialectic is
the greatest end of transcendental philosophy," Kant told the
students of his 1783 metaphysics lecture; "but the analytic
must come first" (29:805). Consequently, the understanding
must precede reason. Otherwise he would have began his
book with the Antinomy chapter, as he explained to Marcus
Herz in a letter accompanying a dedication copy of the first
Critique. This would have guaranteed the book much greater
popularity and would have aroused the curiosity of the
reader, hopelessly trapped in self-contradiction, to comprehend the origin of reason's perplexing illusions. But proper
philosophical methodology requires another procedure.
First, "the ground had to be cleared up" (10:269), and only

by showing how reason builds on the understanding is it possible to show how the illusions of reason arise, and how they can be avoided so that metaphysics can become a body of veritable knowledge.

All this of course remains valid in the *Opus postumum*. Illusions continue to arise when pure theoretical reason ignores the distinction between phenomena and noumena and purports to use its ideas constitutively. When I speak of a reversal of the order of the faculties, therefore, I refer only to the claim that reason, in the *Opus postumum*, must *also* precede the understanding, just as much as the understanding had to precede reason.

To understand this development, let us first distinguish the three major phases of Kant's last work. The first phase is dictated by Kant's realization that there needs to be a special Transition from the metaphysical foundations of natural science to physics, since every investigation that deserves the name of a science must be preceded by an a priori sketch of that science; consequently, there must be something like an a priori elementary system of the moving forces of matter if physics is to be possible as a systematic science. At the same time, during this phase Kant is lacking any 'idea' or 'plan' that he could lay at the basis of the projected science of transition. This situation changes with the ether proofs, since the idea of the ether, as Kant now thinks, contains within itself an elementary system of the moving forces of matter. Consequently, the existence of the ether becomes the supreme principle of the Transition.

What might be called the second phase commences with Kant's realization that the newly found principle of the elementary system does not yet guarantee the real knowability of the moving forces of matter: its 'topic' of concepts does not yet found any experience. Or, in other words, we could not come to know the moving forces of matter if we were not conscious of our own activity in exercising acts of attraction and repulsion. Thus the second phase culminates in the *Selbst-setzungslehre* and ends with the realization that the ideas of practical reason, such as right and duty, also have moving force in nature.

The third phase is marked by the extension of the *Selbst-setzungslehre* to the moral-practical domain, and by a re-evaluation and redefinition of transcendental philosophy as doctrine of ideas, or *Ideenlehre.*

With this development of Kant's thoughts in mind, it may seem natural to assume that it was the ether proofs of the first period that incited Kant to reverse the order of understanding and reason in the *Opus postumum.* The ether, as the basis of all moving forces of matter, does indeed occupy a position similar to that of the *omnitudo realitatis* in Kant's *Nova dilu-cidatio.* And yet such an assumption would be mistaken. The ether, even if it yields a principle for the Transition, would precede the projected *Transition from the Metaphysical Foun-dations of Natural Science to Physics* but would not thereby precede all employment of the understanding. As an ideal, it would presuppose and follow the application of the cate-gories, but the reverse does not hold. Hence it would not necessitate a reversal of the order between reason and under-standing. Such a reversal only becomes necessary, I suggest, with the extension of the *Selbstsetzungslehre* to the moral-practical domain in what I have described as the third phase of Kant's work on the *Opus postumum.* Let us briefly review the basic argument of Kant's twofold *Selbstsetzung.*

In the beginning was—not just for Faust[9] but also for Kant—the deed. Or better still: *my* deed. "The first act of knowledge is the verb: I am,—self-consciousness, for I, [as] subject, am an object to myself. In this, however, there lies a relation which precedes all determination of the subject" (22:413, Op. 179f.). Self-consciousness thus is an act through which the subject makes itself into an object. In or with this original act, two things are given or emerge: (1) a "double" I:

the I as subject and the I as object; and (2) the inscrutable imperative *nosce te ipsum,* which makes it impossible for the thinking I to keep to itself, as it were, and impels it to go beyond the original act of self-consciousness and determine itself to cognition. Since "to determine" means to ascribe a predicate under exclusion of its opposite, I must make myself into an object that can be distinguished from something other—hence from what must be viewed as *given.* This becomes possible, that is, my intuition becomes empirical, insofar as I can think of myself as being *affected.*

Consequently, this first or "merely logical" act of consciousness is followed by a second, this time synthetic, act through which the subject makes itself into an object of intuition: "The second act is to determine this object as pure *a priori intuition* and also as *concept;* that is, [to progress] to knowledge, as the complex *(complexus)* of representations, completely determined according to a principle of the categories . . . and thus to represent the manifold in appearance as belonging to the unity of experience (as existing)" (22:77, Op. 186). This also implies two things: (1) there must be something external, something distinct from me; hence space itself must become perceptible in the sense that I can occupy a position in space to which other things can be external; and (2) I myself must exert moving forces without which no perception would take place, not even that of my own position in space. "To mere outer and inner perception as such there already belong moving forces—of matter outside me as well as of their composition within me" (22:18.13–15). In these acts of determination, the subject constitutes itself as an object of empirical intuition, given in space and time.

That is only one side of the coin, however. For I also posit myself as a person, as a moral being capable of rights and duties. The possibility of this act is also grounded in the original duplication of the I in self-consciousness. As we noticed, Kant defines "person" as a being that not only thinks but also can say to itself, "I think." Through this act I raise myself above nature, and especially above my own sensuous nature. I can view and determine myself from the outside, as it were. I can, in principle, behold myself from an external viewpoint and subject my own actions to an evaluation from another perspective. My own objectification in self-consciousness—the conscious perspective of the first-person singular—permits and makes possible the view of myself from the perspective of a third-person singular. And because the 'I' of the first-person singular—the necessary unity of consciousness—remains numerically the same throughout, I can be held accountable for how I have viewed and treated myself and others. For this reason, in the *Metaphysics of Morals*, Kant defines person as "a subject whose actions can be *imputed* to him" (6:223), and characterizes "imputation" in the moral sense as "the judgment by which someone is regarded as the author *(causa libera)* of an action, which is then called a *deed (factum)* and stands under laws" (6:227). In the *Anthropology*, Kant makes the link between imputability and self-consciousness even more explicit: "The fact that man can have the representation 'I' raises him infinitely above all the other beings living on earth. By this he is a *person*, and by virtue of this unity of consciousness through all the changes he may undergo, he is one and the same person—that is, a being altogether different in rank and dignity from *things*" (7:127).

In virtue of the fact that I can elevate myself above my sensuous nature, I place myself in a higher class, namely, that of autonomous legislating beings, and I am thus (as Kant says) originator of my own rank (see 22:118, Op. 201). Since the fundamental condition of the determination of my own will is the free will of another person, the law of duty follows from the necessary limitation of any finite rational being endowed with a will: "*Every human being* is, in virtue of *his freedom* and of the law which *restricts* it, made subject to necessitation through his moral-practical reason, stands under command and prohibition, and, as man, under the imperative of duty" (22:120, Op. 203). The concept of duty is thus one of the moving forces in the world, and as a human being I am consequently limited by nature and duty alike.

But why, one might ask, do I posit myself in precisely this way, in a twofold way, as thing and as person? In the first fascicle, Kant declares that all philosophy is autognosis and autonomy, that is, science and wisdom, and provides the following elaboration: "Science and wisdom are two entirely different principles of thought. The tendency toward both amounts to two different operations: the former [scil. latter] of the subject merely within itself, the latter [scil. former] outside itself—both according to principles a priori" (21: 106.1–2, 104.3–16). Yet this seems to repeat the problem: The two "entirely different principles" of the subject "within itself" and "outside itself" cannot be derived from the original act of self-consciousness, which according to Kant is a logical proposition. Both are grounded in the duplication of the I in self-consciousness, only to proceed from there in two entirely different directions, and following different rules. How are we to make intelligible these first steps beyond the original 'I am' of self-consciousness?

The problem can also be phrased in another way. "We can know no objects, either within us or as lying outside of us, except insofar as we insert in ourselves the *actus* of cognition, according to certain laws" (21:99, Op. 255), Kant states. But what are these "certain laws"? Where do they come from, and how do I come to know them? What kinds of forces, what "*actus* of cognition," do we have to "insert into ourselves"—prior to any distinction between "inner" and "outer," a distinction itself dependent on these acts of cognition? The logical act of self-consciousness only yields something determining and something determined (something thinking and something thought.) And then? Both need to be determined further. But whence comes the thought that what is determined or thought in the first equation needs to be further determined outwardly, what is determining or thinking needs to be further determined inwardly? Where do the concepts 'inner' and 'outer' come from? And where do such concepts as 'right', 'duty', 'freedom', on the one hand, and 'attraction', repulsion', 'space occupation', on the other, originate? Do they emerge from the conceptual distance between what determines and what is determined? What could be meant here by 'distance'? There is no doubt that we who are already equipped with these concepts can understand what Kant is trying to say. Yet this is not enough. What we need to understand, but do not yet, is how the self-positing and self-determining subject avails itself of these concepts.

It is here, if I am not mistaken, that reason enters the stage and generates two ideas in the production and interpretation of which it constitutes itself as theoretical and practical reason, respectively. More precisely, these are the ideas or ideals of two *maxima*, which allow for a throughgoing determination of appearances and hence permit a first orientation in the determination of myself. These ideals represent "possible forces affecting reason" (21:83, Op. 249) that I must anticipate and whose counteractions I must elicit in order to posit myself. "There are, however, only two active principles which can be thought of as causes of these appearances: God and the world" (21:54, Op. 213). Kant characterizes both *maxima* as "limitless activity with regard to forces," the former, God, as qualitative, according to degree; the latter, the world, as quantitative, according to volume (see 21:11, Op. 219). God is the moral being who has only rights but no duties, who is entitled and has the power to command all and thus unites all rational beings in one moral universe. World is the totality of all empirical objects and of the forces affecting the senses—in other words, the successor to the ether conception of the earlier fascicles.

When Kant now repeatedly asks himself: Where does this scale of ideas come from? he can only answer himself that we must have such ideas if we are to be conscious of ourselves. "The *totality* of beings is a concept given a priori to reason, arising from the consciousness of myself. I must have objects of my thinking and apprehend them; otherwise I am *unconscious* of myself . . . Reason inevitably creates objects for itself. Hence everything that thinks has a God" (21:82f., Op. 248). It is important to note that these ideas do not carry with them any manifold of intuition. The ideas of pure (not empirically determinable) reason, as Kant points out (at 21:84, Op. 250), contribute nothing to what is material but precede formally all appearances in space and time. They found not a science of objects but a "science of forms . . . under which, if they [i.e., objects] were to be given, they had to appear" (21:90.24–26).

We can now give a preliminary answer to the question why, in the *Opus postumum*, Kant thinks that pure reason needs to precede the understanding. Pure reason needs to precede, we might say, because without its projections, thought could take no step into the world—indeed, without reason's ideal of a world, there would not even arise the notion of a sensible outer. Into this world I can then insert moving forces of attraction and repulsion as well as concepts of right and duty, thus progressing to determination and cognition in an infinite series:

> Without transcendental philosophy one can form for oneself no concept as to how, and by what principle, one could design the plan of a system, by which a coherent whole could be established as rational knowledge for reason; yet this must necessarily take place if one would turn rational man into a being who knows himself . . .
>
> Transcendental philosophy precedes the assertion of things that are thought, as their archetype,

[the place] in which they must be set. (21:7,
Op. 256)

I would like to use this last quotation ("Transcendental philosophy precedes the assertion of things that are thought, as
their archetype, [the place] in which they must be set") as a
bridge to a philosopher of the twentieth century, namely,
Ludwig Wittgenstein. A comparison with Wittgenstein, I
think, may shed further light on Kant's conviction that reason must precede the understanding. We can begin by noting
that some of Wittgenstein's statements sound remarkably
similar to Kant's. Here are a few examples:

> Suppose I wanted to replace all the words of my
> language at once by other ones; how could *I* tell
> the *place* where one of the new words belongs? Is it
> images that keep the places of the words? (Z §10;
> second italics mine)

> Perhaps you say: two can only be ostensively de-
> fined in this way: "This number is called 'two'."
> For the word "number" here shews what *place* in
> language, in grammar, we assign to the word
> ... The word "number" in the definition does in-
> deed shew this *place;* does shew the post at which
> we station the word. (PI §29; my italics)

> So one might say: the ostensive definition explains
> the use—the meaning—of the word when the over-
> all role of the word in language is clear ... [The ex-
> planation] only tells him the use, if the *place* is
> already prepared. (PI §§30–1; my italics)

It is easy to overlook the distinction Wittgenstein is making
here between the use and the role of a word, but it is a distinction that is of central importance to the point he is trying
to make. Although the role and use of a word are closely re-

lated, they are by no means identical. Thus, with regard to the term "to read," Wittgenstein notes: "The use of this word in the ordinary circumstances of our life is of course extremely familiar to us. But the role the word plays in our life, and therewith the language game in which we employ it, would be difficult to describe even in rough outline" (PI §156; cf. §182, and PG 68). Yet it is precisely the role a word plays in our language that is at the center of his investigation: "This role is what we need to understand in order to resolve philosophical paradoxes. And hence definitions usually fail to resolve them; and so, *a fortiori* does the assertion that a word is 'indefinable'"(PI §182).

In order to get a clearer idea of the importance Wittgenstein attaches to the roles of words in language, let us turn briefly to where he introduces this term in connection with ostensive definition in the *Philosophical Investigations.*[10] Wittgenstein first discusses a primitive form of language, containing words such as "block," "pillar," "slab," "beam," which are thought of as standing for the objects they name. A child uses such primitive forms of language when it learns to talk, Wittgenstein says, and points out: "Here the teaching of language is not explanation, but training [*Abrichtung*]" (PI §5). He speaks of "training" or, in connection with the teacher's pointing to the object and directing the pupil's attention to it, "ostensive teaching of words" rather than of ostensive explanation or definition, "because the child cannot as yet *ask* what the name is" (PI §6; see §31). It is worth noting that it is in connection with such training that Wittgenstein originally introduces the term "language-game," emphasizing the interwovenness of linguistic and nonlinguistic practices. Before one has mastered such primitive language-games, there can be no understanding of an ostensive definition.

Let us consider one of Wittgenstein's examples. Suppose I do not know what the word "sepia" means and someone points to a particular object, saying: "This is sepia." Do I thereby come to understand what "sepia" means? Is it the name for the color of the object? Or its shape? The material? Or perhaps even a number? Whatever I take it to mean, "an ostensive definition can be variously interpreted in *every* case" (PI §28). For the definition to be unambiguous, I must know that it is a color term that is being explained to me. For the concept 'color' shows what "place in language" the term "sepia" is assigned to; it indicates the "post at which we station the word" (PI §29). Any definition is, at least potentially, an answer to a question by the person to whom the definition is given. Asking a name and ostensive explanation (definition) are correlatives; they are a new (later) language-game. For this reason, Wittgenstein says at §30: "One has already to know (or be able to do) something in order to be capable of asking a thing's name." This presupposes an understanding of the *role* the name is to play, of the "place" it is to occupy within language. Without such prior grasp, no definition can succeed. The ostensive definition explains the use—the meaning—of the word, according to Wittgenstein, "when the overall role of the word is clear. Thus if I know that someone means to explain a color-word to me, the ostensive definition 'That is called "sepia"' will help me to understand the word" (PI §30).

Against this account, Quine objected in his article "Ontological Relativity" that it is not necessary to know in advance what is to be explained in order to grasp the point of an ostensive definition. For instance, that "sepia" is a name of a color word will become clear to me when the words "This is sepia" are accompanied by a variety of samples which all have the same color but differ in all other relevant aspects.[11] Yet this objection, although no doubt correct, does not undermine Wittgenstein's point. To recognize in a particular situation what varies and what remains constant, I have to have a prior grasp of such concepts as color, shape, material, and so on—whether they find expression in the course of the definition or not. In fact, Wittgenstein seems to be drawing on the same point as Quine when in connection with a definition of the number two he remarks: "Whether the word 'number' is necessary in the ostensive definition depends on whether without it the other person takes the definition otherwise than I wish" (PI §29; see also §33).

The relevance of Wittgenstein's inquiry lies somewhere else. Even if I can, when presented with a number of samples, recognize the feature that remains constant and distinguish it from the aspects that vary, we take it for granted in such cases that the samples have been selected so as to make this kind of recognition possible. But the selection of samples has to be done by people who already have a grasp of the role in language of the word to be defined, that is, by people to whom the word would *not* have to be explained. Whether *I* know that "sepia" is a color word or not, any understanding of it is grounded in the understanding of the concept of a color, and thus of the role of the term to be defined. And it is essential to the role of any word that it (the role) cannot itself be defined but has to be learned through training *(Abrichtung)*, by means of examples, imitation, practicing, and so on. "Any explanation has its foundation in training," Wittgenstein says in *Zettel* §419, to which he adds in another place: "Do not believe that you have the concept of color within you because you look at a colored object—however you look. (Any more than you possess the concept of a negative number by having debts.)" (Z §332).

The object itself cannot determine that—or how, or for what—it is to function as a sample. It is not the intrinsic character of the sample but the background of training and instruction, of a shared form of life, against which our general agreement in the roles of terms becomes intelligible. Nature, Wittgenstein never tires of pointing out, does not force any particular interpretation on us; it does not determine how we carve it up. The saying that the rules of grammar are arbitrary is introduced precisely to prevent this kind of misunderstanding: "Grammar tells what kind of object anything is" (PI §373; see Z §331, §320).

This is one important result of Wittgenstein's inquiries. The other one is this: I cannot fix the role of a word by myself. It is easy enough to see why this must be so. If an understanding of the role of a word, its "place in language," is a precondition of the definition of that word, if, furthermore, a grasp of the role presupposes training and confrontation with selected samples, then I cannot give an ostensive definition to myself. For in that case, I myself would have to select the relevant samples. Yet I could do so only if I already knew the meaning of the word to be explained (which is not the case). In other words, the object must be a sample for the explanation of the word, and at the same time the explanation must make the particular object a sample. Word and sample thus require and support each other *idem per idem,* and hence not at all: first the object is to give meaning to the name, then the name is to be used to determine what kind of experience I am having. Thus, in his "Notes for Lectures on 'Private Experience' and 'Sense Data,'" Wittgenstein writes with regard to an inner experience that is to serve as the ground of a private definition: "The private experience is to serve as a paradigm, and at the same time admittedly it can't be a paradigm."[12]

Let us now, with this Wittgensteinian background in mind, return to Kant's claims about the function of reason in the *Opus postumum.* There are of course substantial differences between their respective views. Nevertheless, I believe that Wittgenstein's inquiries can also shed light on Kant's problem. To say it right out, my thesis is that Kant's placement of reason antecedent to understanding is motivated by considerations similar to those that motivate Wittgenstein's discussion of the roles of words. I want to illustrate this thesis with three examples.

First, just as Wittgenstein lets all language—and hence in a certain way all thought—begin with the learning of the roles of words, Kant lets all thought emerge originally from the fundamental ideas of reason. He speaks of a faculty or power of thinking *(Denkungsvermögen)* which is not yet "substance" (21:32, Op. 235) but which must give form to itself in order to come to know itself: "Ideas are self-created subjective principles of the power of thought ... of a reason which constitutes itself into a thought-object" (21:29, 27, Op. 231–233). Were it not for its ideas, the power of thought would be without orientation: "to give one's self-created ideas form, extension and limits, from which ideas all original thought emerges" (21:88.27–28). Kant's ideas, like Wittgenstein's roles, contribute nothing to what is material in knowledge, but provide the forms, prepare the places or topoi at which objects—or words—can be put. Kant's *Ideenlehre* is a science not of objects but "of forms ... under which, if they [i.e., objects] were to be given, they had to appear" (21: 90.24–26; see also 21:8.19–21).

And Wittgenstein says: "What has to be accepted, the given, is—so one could say—*forms of life*" (PI, p. 226e). Yet the fictitious internal interlocutor with whom Wittgenstein was engaged in a lifelong argument finds this hard to accept. Doesn't one for example put the primary colors together, Wittgenstein lets him ask, because there is a similarity between them? Or at least put *colors* together and contrast them with shapes and notes, because there is a similarity between them? And doesn't this classification describe the world as it really is? To which Wittgenstein replies: "When I set this up as the right way of dividing up the world, have I a pre-conceived idea in my head as a paradigm? Of which in that case I can only say: 'Yes, that is the kind of way we look at things'" (Z §331; see PG §143). "The rules of grammar cannot be justified by shewing that their application makes a representation agree with reality. For this justification would itself have to describe what is represented" (PG §134). Neither Wittgenstein's roles nor Kant's ideas are derived from nature. Both, roles as well as ideas, are emphatically normative in character; they are not descriptive. Kant even goes so far as to characterize Newtonian attraction through empty space and human freedom as analogous concepts, namely, as "categorical imperatives—*ideas*" (21:35, Op. 237; see 21:51, Op. 242, and 21:70.26–31).

My second point of comparison between Kant and Wittgenstein concerns the distinctions 'inner-outer' and 'subjective-objective'. According to my interpretation, for Kant these distinctions are in the end grounded in the two ideas of God and World. The forms of sensibility as such do not yield an outer or an inner. As Kant now emphasizes repeatedly, outer and inner perceptions require moving forces which I generate in accordance with an idea: "We can know no objects, either in us or as lying outside us, except insofar as we insert in ourselves the *actus* of cognition, according to certain laws" (21:99, Op. 255). Accordingly, Kant characterizes space and time not simply as forms of intuition, as he had done in the first *Critique,* but as "forms of our effective forces" *(Formen unserer Wirkungskräfte)* (21:38.14), or as "acts of the power of representation positing itself" (22:88, Op. 193; see also 22:41, Op. 178).

Here the comparison with Wittgenstein is especially interesting. I am thinking primarily of the compelling reflections in *Zettel* §§409ff., in which Wittgenstein tries to show that any description of a subjective experience—and hence the distinction 'in me–outside me'—presupposes a grasp of the role of those words in which the experience is to be expressed. Here we may have the most important difference between the positions of Kant and Wittgenstein. For Wittgenstein tries to show that, just as one can make mistakes in calculation only after one has learned how to calculate, and can doubt only if one already knows something, likewise one can speak of a subjective experience only in a being that already has objective experience. Here, too, understanding the role of words precedes: I have to know what, for instance, the word "red" means before I can say, "That appears to be red," or, "That looks red to me." Wittgenstein tries to establish this point in a number of aphorisms. In §420, for instance, he writes: "'It looks red to me.'—'And what is red like?'—'Like *this.*' Here the right paradigm must be pointed to." And in §422 he asks: "Why doesn't one teach a child the language-game 'It looks red to me' from the first? Because it is not yet able to understand the rather fine distinction between seeming and being?" To which he gives himself the answer: "The red visual impression is a new *concept.* The language-game that we teach him then is: 'It looks to me . . . , it looks to you . . . ' In the first language-game a person does not occur as perceiving subject" (Z §423f.).

If in the first language game a person as perceiving subject does not occur, neither does a sentence of the form '*x* is in me.' Self-ascriptions of this type are later achievements, are new concepts, as Wittgenstein says. A subjective perspective can be gained only in an objective world.[13]

My third point of comparison is also the last one. For Wittgenstein, roles determine the grammatical place at which words can be placed, and thus their possible use and their meaning. Hence they must be given prior to any explanation of a word. Nevertheless, they are not extracted from the nature of things but are determined by our shared form of life; hence they are laid down by humans. Learning a language becomes possible through something that has been fixed by us, yet which to the one who learns must necessarily have the character of something given. The shared form of life, and with it the grammatical places of words and their roles in language, is thus both given and arbitrary.

Now, I find it fascinating that Kant, when discussing the ideals of reason in the *Opus postumum,* struggles with the problem that, while they are thought-entities or subjective forms, they also have to be regarded at the same time as given and as independent of the subject. That can be shown for the idea of God and its associated ideas as well as for the idea of the world and its associated ideas. For instance: "God is not a being outside me but merely a thought within me" (21:145.3). At the same time, Kant argues that reason could not consti-tute itself as a practical faculty if it did not assume a highest being outside itself that obligates everyone: "A command, to which everyone must absolutely give obedience, is to be re-garded by everyone as from a being which rules and governs over all. Such a being, as moral, however, is called God. So there is a God" (22:127, Op. 207).

A similar polarity marks the discussion of the ideal of the world. Thus Kant says: "World is the existence . . . of things outside us" (21:39.3–4). At the same time, he explains: "That there is something else outside is my own product" (22:82, Op. 189).[14] And this kind of polarity or duality of aspect we of course already found in Kant's discussion of the ether. On the one hand, Kant claimed that the actuality of the ether could be proved "outside the idea" (21:559.19), since in this one case *a posse ad esse valet consequentia* (21:592.11); on the other hand, Kant insisted that the ether existed only "in idea" (21:553, Op. 82), and was "only a thought-object *(ens rationis)*" (21:231, Op. 77). With regard to objects such as these that condition the collective unity of a possible experi-ence, we have to view them as thought a priori and yet, at the same time, as given (22:377, Op. 119). That is, as transcenden-tal philosophers, we are "spectators and, at the same time, originators" (22:421, Op. 184).

~◊~

If I am not entirely mistaken in my thesis that Kant, in his last work, lets reason precede the understanding because he struggles with a problem that is related to Wittgenstein's problem of the grammatical role of a word, then it is also the case that Wittgenstein's result poses a challenge for a philo-sophical interpretation of the *Ideenlehre* in the *Opus postu-mum.* For it is Wittgenstein's central insight that I cannot determine for myself the roles of words in a language; I can-not, in other words, constitute myself as a linguistic being. Correspondingly, an autonomous act in Kant's sense in which reason constitutes itself in the formulation of its own ideas would philosophically be equally unintelligible.

It may be that Kant saw or suspected something like this. In the end, he seems to assume that something precedes even my own reason—something that he alternatively describes as a "spirit" dwelling in man (22:56, Op. 214), as *"deus in nobis"* (22:130, Op. 209), as "God, the inner vital spirit of man in the world" (21:41, Op. 240), and also as "the unity of this supreme being [*die Einigkeit dieses Allerhöchsten*] that con-stitutes itself and is incomprehensible to itself" (21:135.5–6). On the wrapper of the first fascicle, finally, Kant noted: "If this concept [of God] were not postulated as spirit of the universe there would be no transcendental philosophy" (21: 4.23.24). Such a postulate, clearly, would no longer be a pos-tulate in the sense of the *Critique of Practical Reason,* speci-fying a condition of the "achievability" of moral actions. It could not be regarded simply as the inseparable corollary of an a priori valid practical law. As the ground of the funda-mental divisions underlying transcendental philosophy, this "spirit of the universe" would have to be the ground of theo-retical and practical reason alike, and hence of all laws of thought and action. Ultimately, it would have to be regarded as the ground of consciousness itself.

This thought brings Kant in the end into surprising prox-imity to Hölderlin, for whom it is a "necessary *Willkür* of Zeus" (StA 4:269) from which all oppositions and divisions of conscious life spring. Yet this act of *Willkür* Hölderlin de-cisively located on the other side of *Urtheilung*—and with it on the other side of all philosophical theory. Only poetry can, according to Hölderlin, hope to achieve the goal of eluci-dating primordial being. His philosophical friends Schelling and Hegel eventually parted company with him on precisely this point and began to develop, at the same time that Kant was occupied with the last fascicle, their theories of a philo-sophical, rational cognition of the absolute.

To speculate how Kant's thoughts might have developed had he lived longer can only be a futile exercise. His recorded thoughts come to an end here, on the wrapper of the first fas-cicle. Whether the "postulate" of a spirit of the universe can suffice to secure the fundamental distinctions of transcenden-tal philosophy, or whether, perhaps, a social, intersubjective practice (in Wittgenstein's or any other sense) may be re-quired, Kant could no longer ask. In the end, he could merely point in the direction of problems that would became a cen-tral concern to philosophy especially in the twentieth cen-tury, in connection with questions of a general theory of meaning.

The *Opus postumum* thus occupies a unique place within Kant's ouevre. While marking the true culmination of Kant's philosophical life, it is open-ended as much as it is "unfin-ished." It not only brings to a conclusion problems that oc-cupied Kant throughout most of his career, but in the end it also points beyond itself in the direction of new and unex-plored problems. And while illustrating for us the astonish-ing complexities and inner dynamics of Kant's transcendental *philosophy*, the *Opus postumum* at the same time takes us up to what may be one of the limits of transcendental *idealism*.

Notes

Index

Notes

ONE The Idea of a Transition

1. In a review of Karen Gloy, *Die Kantische Theorie der Naturwissenschaft* (Berlin: de Gruyter, 1976), in *Kant-Studien* 71 (1980), 373.

2. Burkhard Tuschling, *Metaphysische und transzendentale Dynamik in Kants opus postumum* (Berlin: de Gruyter, 1971), p. 46.

3. See Kant's letter to J. S. Beck, October 16, 1792, (11:375f.).

4. Tuschling, *Dynamik*, p. 6.

5. Vittorio Mathieu, *Kants Opus postumum*, ed. Gerd Held (Frankfurt am Main: Klostermann, 1989), pp. 42f. Mathieu oddly misreads the last phrase "as if the understanding [*der Verstand*] contained the ground of unity" although he quotes the Kantian passage from which this is taken on the same page: "as if an understanding [*ein Verstand*] (though it be not ours) had supplied them [i.e., particular empirical laws] for the benefit of our cognitive faculties, so as to render possible a system of experience" (5:180). This conflation of our understanding with a divine understanding suggests that Mathieu misinterprets what exactly is subjective in Kant's principle of a formal purposiveness of na-

ture—a suggestion that will receive additional confirmation shortly.

6. Ibid., p. 41.

7. Michael Friedman, *Kant and the Exact Sciences* (Cambridge, Mass.: Harvard University Press, 1992), pp. 237, 238, 240.

8. The reasons for Kant's reaction are spelled out in Chapter 3.

9. In particular, it makes untenable Tuschling's contention that in 1792 Kant "did not yet think of such a 'Transition'" and that there is no reliable evidence for it prior to 1795 (see Tuschling, *Dynamik*, p. 31).

10. This discovery must have occurred at about the time when Kant was preparing the second edition of the *Critique of Pure Reason* for publication. This is suggested by the revised footnote at B25–26, and by the fact that the catalogue for the Leipzig book fair of Easter 1787 already announced a *Groundwork for a Critique of Taste* by Kant (see 10:488, 490, 514).

11. "This concept [of nature's subjective purposiveness for the power of judgment] does not allow us to cognize or prove anything concerning the object because it is in itself indeterminable and inadequate for knowledge" (5:340).

12. Friedman, *Kant and the Exact Sciences,* pp. 251–253. See also p. 48: "The doctrine of the regulative use of the ideas of reason becomes the doctrine of reflective judgment in the third *Critique.*" Friedman is of course not alone in holding this view. It has almost become a commonplace in the literature. On this point, even such fundamentally different interpreters of Kant as Friedman, Paul Guyer, and Henry Allison seem to agree. See Paul Guyer, "Reason and Reflective Judgment: Kant on the Significance of Systematicity," in *Nous* 24 (1990), 17: "In the *Critique of Judgment,* however, published only three years after the revised second edition of the *Critique of Pure Reason,* the regulative ideal of systematicity is reassigned to the newly introduced faculty of reflective judgment." Fundamentally the same view is endorsed by Henry Allison in "Is the *Critique of Judgment* 'Post-critical'?" in Sally Sedgwick, ed., *The Reception of Kant's Philosophy: Fichte, Schelling, and Hegel,* (New York: Cambridge University Press, forthcoming).

13. Friedman, *Kant and the Exact Sciences,* p. 253f. See also p. 254: "It is entirely obscure how this new autonomous sta-

tus [of reflective judgment] can possibly account for the Transition project."

14. Ibid., p. 265.

15. We demand agreement "as a sort of duty" (5:296, 353), according to Kant, because of the analogy of beauty with the morally good, in which we cannot but have an interest as rational beings. With regard to objects of taste, the faculty of judgment is autonomous and gives a law to itself, just as reason does with regard to the faculty of desire.

16. Kant expresses this problem with rare clarity in this passage: "Physics as a system requires a principle of how one is to investigate methodically the moving forces of nature, divide them into classes, and thus is to be guided with regard to the coordination of the whole. For this a priori concepts of the moving forces are needed, however, which indicate [*hinweisen auf*] the composition of those forces for the sake of experience. It must be possible to enumerate them completely; and none of them must be derived from physics, because physics itself must expect from them its own establishment [*Errichtung*]" (22:265.1–8).

17. On this point, see my "Kant's Notion of Philosophy," *Monist* 72:2 (1988), 285–304.

18. The English edition of Kant's *Opus postumum,* because it had to be an abridged edition of Kant's text, can convey only a limited sense of the repetitiveness and experimental nature of these early drafts.

19. I here ignore the differences between caloric and ether, since in these drafts of the *Opus postumum* Kant either uses both terms interchangeably, or regards caloric simply as a modification of the ether (light being another one).

20. It is worth noting, however, that Kant here, in two marginal notes, for the first time relates caloric to modality, even if only with respect to its problematic state of aggregation: "4th Category. Caloric is not a fluid, yet it makes everything fluid." And: "4th Category. Of caloric in general; whether it be subsisting or inhering. Principle of modality" (21:282.22; 288.28).

21. See Johann Samuel Traugott Gehler, *Physicalisches Wörterbuch oder Versuch einer Erklärung der vornehmsten Begriffe und Kunstwörter der Naturlehre* (Leipzig: im Schwickertschen Verlage, 1785–95), 2:565–576 ("Hebel"). Gehler recites the history of the problem from Archimedes to

d'Alembert and concludes: "Concerning the inadequacies of the proofs of the first law of statics, d'Alembert rightly remarked (*Traité de Dynamique*, à Paris, 1743, préface) that one had been more concerned with enlarging the system of mechanics than with illuminating its foundations; one always proceeded with this without sufficiently securing its ground. Herr Hofrat Kästner (*Vectis et compositionis virum theoria evidentius exposita,* Lips. 1753) finally overcame this deficiency and offered a fully convincing proof for the law of the lever." See also Gehler's article "Zusammensetzung der Kräfte und Bewegungen," ibid., 4:931.

22. Erich Adickes, *Kants Opus postumum dargestellt und beurteilt* (Berlin: Reuther & Reichard, 1920), p. 118.

23. Before we accept Tuschling's radical thesis that Kant, in his *Opus postumum,* reduced the entire *Metaphysical Foundations* to phoronomy, it might be worth considering if Kant's repeated claim that this text had not treated of moving forces is not to be understood in the sense of the passage cited previously, namely, that the *Metaphysical Foundations* had furnished "no specifically determined," that is, empirically demonstrable moving forces of matter "of which one could know whether they exist in nature (22:282, Op. 100), but only "attraction and repulsion in general" (21:363.1–2). Although these are, in a way, moving forces, they cannot be experienced as such. Consequently, "attraction and repulsion in general" are not moving forces in the sense of the Transition; only their empirically encounterable *specific* modifications are: "If we are to take a step from the metaphysical foundations of natural science to physics we have to see that we can presuppose the existence of certain moving forces of attraction and repulsion" (22:264.11–15). One such specific force is cohesion, which is required for the formation of a physical *body* (see 21:378, Op. 12). On my interpretation, then, the *Metaphysical Foundations of Natural Science* would have been a theory of matter, not just phoronomy, but (contrary to Kant's own assertion) not a *doctrine of body* (see 4:477.15; 478.1 and 7). Consequently, "in this transition from the metaphysical foundations of natural science to physics there is [also] that from matter to the formation of bodies" (22:282, Op. 100).

24. Gehler, *Physicalisches Wörterbuch,* 2:575f.

TWO The "Green Color of a Lawn"
and Kant's Theory of Matter

1. *Kants Nachlaßwerk und die Kritik der Urteilskraft* (1939), reprinted in Gerhard Lehmann, *Beiträge zur Geschichte und Interpretation der Philosophie Kants* (Berlin: de Gruyter, 1968), pp. 295–373.

2. Ibid., pp. 295–297.

3. Ibid., pp. 370f.

4. See Vittorio Mathieu, *La filosofia trascendentale e l'OP di Kant* (Turin: Edizioni di "Filosofia," 1958), and *Kants Opus postumum* (Frankfurt am Main: Klostermann, 1989).

5. Lehmann, *Beiträge,* p. 371; Mathieu, *Kants Opus postumum,* p. 240.

6. Of course, this does not rule out the possibility that Kant requested a correction to be made in the third edition.

7. The *human* organism is mentioned briefly only in the Doctrine of Method of the Critique of Teleological Judgment. There, however, Kant's discussion shifted to another topic: ethico-theology and the final end of nature.

8. "The concept of organic bodies (which contain a vital principle) already presupposes experience: For, without the latter, the very idea of organic bodies would be an empty concept (without example). But man has in his own self an example of an understanding which contains moving forces, which determine a body according to laws" (22:481, Op. 137).

9. This passage is discussed at some length—yet without reference to the *Opus postumum*—in Theodore E. Uehling, Jr., *The Notion of Form in Kant's Critique of Aesthetic Judgment* (The Hague: Mouton, 1971), pp. 22–34.

10. *L. Euleri opuscula varii argumenti* (Berlin: Haude & Spener, 1746), 1:169–244, §22.

11. All that Kant concedes is that its assumption is "not impossible" (4:534).

12. This volume came out in 1796 and was subtitled "The One Possible Standpoint from Which Critical Philosophy Is to Be Judged." It eventually led to a break between Kant and Beck. Volumes 1 and 2 were published in 1793 and 1794, respectively.

13. Erich Adickes, in his commentary on Volume 14 of the Academy edition, thought there was no escape from Kant's

circle (14:338), but subsequently changed his mind and alleged that the circle was only one of Kant's wording, not one in substance (see Erich Adickes, *Kant als Naturforscher* [Berlin: de Gruyter, 1924], p. 215). Thus we are to assume that Kant misunderstood himself when he confessed to Beck that he did not know how to avoid the circle. Burkhard Tuschling, by contrast, thinks that the circle in Kant's theory of matter eventually led him to disregard the entire *Metaphysical Foundations,* with the sole exception of its first chapter on "Phoronomy," as worthless (see his *Metaphysische und transzendentale Dynamik in Kants opus postumum* [Berlin: de Gruyter, 1971], pp. 90–122)—a view I disagree with for reasons given in Chapter 1. Tuschling's interpretation is also endorsed by Kenneth R. Westphal in "Kant's Dynamical Constructions," *Journal of Philosophical Research* 20 (1995), 381–429. Jules Vuillemin, "Kant's 'Dynamics': Comments on Tuschling and Förster," in Eckart Förster, ed., *Kant's Transcendental Deductions: The Three Critiques and the Opus postumum* (Stanford: Stanford University Press, 1989), p. 243, points out that no given quantity of matter is presupposed when Kant introduces the fundamental force of attraction as one of the two forces by which a space is filled. Thus the definition of matter is not circular, and Kant "was mistaken" if he thought otherwise. This is of course correct, but it is not the *definition* of matter that Kant expresses concerns about in his letter to Beck, but the explanation of the differences in density, hence the constructability of the concept of matter. And to construct this concept in pure intuition, more is needed than the definition of the two fundamental forces. Michael Friedman, unfortunately, decided to ignore Kant's diagnosis of a circle in the dynamical theory of matter altogether: "Since Kant never refers to the supposed circularity in question in the *Opus* itself, it is hard to see how this problem can have fundamental importance for the *Transition* project" (*Kant and the Exact Sciences* [Cambridge, Mass.: Harvard University Press, 1992], p. 223fn.). Is this really so hard to see? This problem would have fundamental importance for the Transition project if the success of the Transition itself depended on Kant's solution of the circle problem, that is, his revised matter theory. And since, in that case, the Transition *presupposed* this solution, the lack of explicit references to the problem would hardly be surprising. (I also believe that there are enough implicit references in the text so as to establish the connection that Friedman finds missing; see, e.g., pp. 87–88.)

14. See Martin Carrier, *The Completeness of Scientific Theories* (Dordrecht: Kluwer Academic Publishers, 1994), esp. pp. 194–202. I am indebted to Martin Carrier for several helpful discussions of the circle in Kant's theory of matter.

15. Erich Adickes, *Kants Opus postumum dargestellt und beurteilt* (Berlin: Reuther & Reichard, 1920), p. 37.

16. See Albert Landau, ed., *Rezensionen zur Kantischen Philosophie, 1781–87* (Bebra: Albert Landau Verlag, 1991). On May 14, 1787, Daniel Jenisch wrote to Kant: "To date your *Foundations of Natural Science* has not been read much, and those who read it found it more difficult than the *Critique* itself, with the exception of the chapter on the deduction" (10:486).

17. *Göttingische Anzeigen von gelehrten Sachen* (December 1786), 1916. See also 21:415, Op. 3. That Kästner is the author of the anonymous review is clear from Oscar Fambach, *Die Mitarbeiter der Göttingischen Gelehrten Anzeigen, 1769–1836* (Tübingen: Universitätsbibliothek, 1976), p. 134.

18. *Journal der Physik* 7 (1793), 208–237.

19. For a more detailed discussion of various theories of matter in Kant's time, see the excellent article by Martin Carrier, "Kants Theorie der Materie und ihre Wirkung auf die zeitgenössische Chemie," *Kant-Studien* 81 (1990), 170–210, esp. 176–180.

20. Franz von Baader, *Über das pythagoräische Quadrat in der Natur, oder die vier Weltgegenden* (Tübingen: Cotta, 1798).

21. *Friedrich Wilhelm Joseph von Schelling's sämmtliche Werke,* ed. K. F. A. Schelling (Stuttgart: I. G. Cotta'scher Verlag, 1857), 2:241; English translation by Errol E. Harris and Peter Heath (Cambridge: Cambridge University Press, 1988), p. 192. Schelling here credits Franz von Baader's *Über das pythagoräische Quadrat* with first expressing this critique of Kant. In fact, with regard to the first edition of Schelling's *Ideas,* Baader had already written to F. H. Jacobi on February 8, 1798: "Schelling I know, but I am not at all pleased with him. If, in the knowledge of matter, one has finally reached the point of acknowledging the inner

conflict or the two opposing fundamental forces or natures [of matter], then it is indeed unforgivable to ignore the third, in which and through which those two alone can be active, and which, separating and dividing them, nevertheless holds them *together* (because they can never truly become one)." (*Franz von Baader's sämmtliche Werke,* ed. Franz Hoffmann [Leipzig: Hermann Bethmann, 1857], 15:181.)

22. *Schelling's sämmtliche Werke,* Bd. 4:26.

23. Ibid., 4:27.

24. Ibid., 3:103fn.

25. Ibid., 4:29.

26. In his obituary of Kant in the *Fränkische Staats- und Gelehrtenzeitung* 49/50 (March 1804), Schelling mentions that in 1801 Kant was still working on a book, "Transition from Metaphysics to Physics," which would have been "of the highest interest" if Kant had lived to finish it, but he gives no indication of any knowledge of its contents (*Schelling's sämmtliche Werke,* 6:8). For Kant's potential knowledge of Schelling, see Op. 274–275, note 89.

THREE The "Gap" in Kant's Critical Philosophy

1. It is important to note that in 1786 Kant is convinced of having provided a metaphysical *doctrine of body,* not just a dynamical theory of matter that leaves untouched the question how matter forms a body.

2. Kuno Fischer, *Das Streber- und Gründerthum in der Literatur: Vademecum für Herrn Pastor Krause in Hamburg* (Stuttgart: Verlag der Cottaschen Buchhandlung, 1884), p. 33.

3. Kuno Fischer, *Geschichte der neuern Philosophie* (Mannheim: Verlagsbuchhandlung von Friedrich Wassermann, 1860), 3:83.

4. Erich Adickes, *Kants Opus postumum dargestellt und beurteilt* (Berlin: Reuter & Reichard, 1920), p. 162.

5. Gerhard Lehmann, "Das philosophische Grundproblem in Kants Nachlaßwerk," *Blätter für deutsche Philosophie* 2:1 (1937), 60; reprinted in G. Lehmann, *Beiträge zur Geschichte und Interpretation der Philosophie Kants* (Berlin: de Gruyter, 1969), p. 275.

6. I first did so in 1987 in my article "Is There 'A Gap' in Kant's Critical System?" on which the present chapter is partly based. Subsequently, Michael Friedman has offered an interpretation of the "gap" that accepts my criticism of the identification of "gap" and "transition" but explains the former in a fundamentally different way (see his *Kant and the Exact Sciences* [Cambridge, Mass.: Harvard University Press, 1992], esp. pp. 254–264). Although I cannot agree with Friedman's own interpretation (for reasons that will become clear later), I am grateful for his unflagging insistence that my original account of the "gap" in Kant's system was not good enough.

7. Kiesewetter arrived in Königsberg on Michaelmas Day (September 29), 1790 (see 11:267); on November 9 he was already back in Berlin (see 11:233). About Kiesewetter's visit to Kant (his second), there is little but confusion in the literature. Gerhard Lehmann has Kiesewetter staying "for one year" in Königsberg. See his "Bemerkungen zu dem Brief Kants an Kiesewetter vom 27. [*sic*; 25 is correct] März 1790," in *Kant-Studien* 55 (1964), 244; reprinted in his *Kants Tugenden* (Berlin: de Gruyter, 1980), p. 181. Erich Adickes— following F. W. Schubert's (mis)lead in Karl Rosenkranz and Friedrich Wilhelm Schubert's edition of Kant's works (vol. 11, p. 260)—even dates the visit "in 1791" (*Kants Opus postumum*, p. 1). The confusion started with Kiesewetter's first biographer, C. G. Flittner, according to whom Kiesewetter spent "three extremely happy months in Königsberg." See Flittner's "Biographie Johann Gottfried Christian Kiesewetter's," in J. G. C. Kiesewetter, *Darstellung der wichtigsten Wahrheiten der kritischen Philosophie*, 4th amended ed. (Berlin: Flittner'sche Buchhandlung, 1824), p. xvii.; reprinted in *Aetas Kantiana* (1968).

8. Cited in A. Warda, "Eine nachgelassene Arbeit über Kants Naturphilosophie von seinem Schüler Kiesewetter," *Altpreußische Forschungen* 5 (1928), 310. I am grateful to Werner Stark of Marburg for drawing my attention to this article, and to Marian Zwiercan of the Bibliotheka Jagiellonska in Cracow for providing me with a microfilm of Kiesewetter's Preface and Introduction.

9. Kiesewetter had published with Kant's publisher a *Grundriß einer allgemeinen Logik nach Kantischen Grundsätzen*

(Berlin: F. T. Lagarde, 1791), in which he made liberal use of material Kant had unwittingly "dictated" to him (see 11:267, 254). Kant, who himself had plans for a *Logic* as a compendium to his lectures, was infuriated, especially because he learned of this book not through Kiesewetter himself but through their publisher. Kant wrote again only after Kiesewetter sent him as a peace offering a small cask of Teltower Rüben—white carrots of which Kant was particularly fond.

10. See Kant's letter to J. H. Lambert, December 31, 1765 (10:56), and especially Kant's "Nachrichten von der Einrichtung seiner Vorlesungen in dem Winterhalbenjahre, 1765-1766" (2:305-313). "The critique . . . of all philosophy," Kant says here, can have its place only "at the end" (2:310). See also Kant's "new plan" in the "Metaphysik Herder" (28:157).

11. For a different view, see P. Plaass, *Kants Theorie der Naturwissenschaft* (Göttingen: Vandenhoeck & Ruprecht, 1965), pp. 15f., and B. Tuschling, *Metaphysische und transzendentale Dynamik in Kants opus postumum* (Berlin: de Gruyter, 1971), pp. 37f., who both see the work of 1786 as the *realization* of Kant's plan of 1765 to write metaphysical foundations of natural science.

12. The *Metaphysical Foundations* presupposes "the separate (although in itself empirical) concept" of matter (4:472); see also A848.

13. See A145, "The schemata are . . . nothing but a priori determinations of time," and A139, "Thus an application of the category to appearances becomes possible by means of the transcendental determination of time."

14. That the Schematism requires a supplementation of the kind described here has also been suggested by Charles Parsons, "Remark on Pure Natural Science," in Allen W. Wood, ed., *Self and Nature in Kant's Philosophy* (Ithaca: Cornell University Press, 1984), pp. 216-227.

15. This point is also emphasized by Friedman, *Kant and the Exact Sciences,* p. 259: "Without the *Metaphysical Foundations,* therefore, we would have no conception whatsoever of *how* the principles of pure understanding are actually constitutive with respect to experience."

16. See E. Stäbler, *George Berkeleys Auffassung und Wirkung in der Deutschen Philosophie bis Hegel* (Zeulenroda: Bernhard Sporn, 1935), pp. 41–43. Kant's *Critique* was reviewed in the *Göttingischen Gelehrten Anzeigen,* January 19, 1782, pp. 40–48.

17. See 4:469 and also 4:481: "If I am to explicate the concept of matter not by a predicate that applies to it as object but only by its relation to the faculty of cognition in which the representation can first of all be given to me, then matter is every object of the external senses; and this would be its mere metaphysical explanation . . . In contrast to form, matter would be what in external intuition is an object of sensation and consequently would be the properly empirical part of sensible and external intuition, because it cannot be given at all a priori".

18. "Impenetrability, as the fundamental property of matter whereby it first reveals itself to our outer senses as something real in space" (4:508), is thus the empirical datum from which the analysis must proceed.

19. For an excellent discussion of Kant's early theory of matter, see Michael Friedman's Introduction to his *Kant and the Exact Sciences.*

20. Correctly speaking, Kant insists, the difficulty is only a "misunderstanding" [*Mißdeutung*] of the construction in question (4:522).

21. For a different reading of these passages, see Friedman, *Kant and the Exact Sciences,* p. 195, note 45: Referring first to the "difficulty" mentioned in the text as Kant's "considerable diffidence about the prospects for this . . . construction" of the "dynamical concept of matter (from the interplay of attractive and repulsive force)," he then continues: "Indeed, in view of Kant's explicit assertion in the General Observation to Dynamics that the dynamical concept of matter *cannot* be constructed . . . such a diffidence is entirely appropriate." But even in the passage from the General Observation (4:525.7–12) to which Friedman refers his readers, Kant speaks explicitly of "the *specific variety* of matter" and of the impossibility to construct "this [!] concept of matter"—not the concept of matter in general.

22. See Galileo Galilei, *Dialogues concerning Two New Sciences* (New York: Macmillan, 1914), pp. 17–18.

23. The gap is from now on mentioned several times, especially in the "Farrago" sheets of the sixth fascicle: 21:626.10, 637.1, 640.4, 642.19, and 22:182.23

24. A very different account of the "gap" is given by Michael Friedman in his *Kant and the Exact Sciences.* According to Friedman, the "gap" in Kant's critical philosophy opens up between, on the one hand, the constitutive role the *Metaphysical Foundations* plays in providing a priori foundations for Newtonian science, and, on the other hand, the regulative function of reflective judgment when it seeks to organize the particulars of our experience into classes and species, aiming at the ideal of a maximally unified science. For we have no reason, Friedman claims, to assume that both procedures will converge: "The problem of a possible 'gap' is just this: What reason is there to suppose that there is any connection whatsoever between the constitutive procedure of the *Metaphysical Foundation* and the regulative procedure of reflective judgment? Why, in following the regulative maxims of reflective judgment, should we necessarily proceed in the direction of the *Metaphysical Foundations* and the theory of universal gravitation?" (p. 256). We have "no principle whatsoever" for coordinating the two procedures, and no "assurance" that our empirical systematization as guided by reflective judgment will "aim asymptotically at this particular, already given, empirical concept," that is, the concept of matter of the *Metaphysical Foundations* (p. 257). What is more, Friedman draws the remarkable consequence that this problem could not be solved even by "dropping the *Metaphysical Foundations* from the critical system." The problem would simply reappear as a gap between the regulative maxims of reflective judgment and the constitutive principles of the Analytic of the first *Critique.* Because the concept of nature in general that the Analytic specifies is not entirely indeterminate but subject to the three Analogies, and hence to specific conditions of substantiality, causal determination and reciprocity, "there appears to be no more guarantee that the regulative procedures of reflective judgment must always be in harmony with an ideal complete science embodying the general conceptions embodied in the transcendental principles of the understanding than there is analogously in the case of the more specific principles artic-

ulated in the *Metaphysical Foundations*" (p. 259). Now, since Friedman does not recognize any fundamental difference between the principle of reflective judgment and the regulative ideas of reason in the first *Critique,* does it not follow that this gap must already have existed in 1781, between the Analytic and the Appendix to the Dialectic, hence between the understanding and reason?

But how could this be? When describing the regulative employment of the ideas of reason, Kant points out that reason is "never in immediate relation to an object, but only to the understanding" (A643), and that it is the latter's possible empirical acts alone that reason attempts to systematize (A664). Reason can reflect only on what has been constituted previously in accordance with the transcendental principles of the understanding. Thus there cannot be a missing connection (hence a potential gap) between the procedures of the two respective faculties, for if there were, reason/judgment would have no object of outer sense to reflect upon. (If, however, the gap is supposed to be between two *empirical* theories of nature, such as Newtonian mechanics and an alternative to it, then this cannot constitute a gap in the *critical* system of Kant's philosophy.)

Moreover, it does not seem that Friedman can make at all plausible why Kant first noticed the gap in his system in 1798. This is the explanation he gives: "Why then does Kant only first mention the 'gap' in 1798–99? It appears from our above discussion of loose-leafs 6, 3/4, and 5 that Kant had first envisioned an extension of the *Metaphysical Foundations* that was to have proceeded purely mathematically—on the basis of the purely mathematical unity of all possible moving forces in space. He then came to see, however, that a fundamentally different type of unity—that of reflective judgment (natural investigation) is required. It is therefore at this point, and only at this point, that the idea of a possible extension of the constitutive procedure of the *Mathematical Foundations* is self-consciously and deliberately juxtaposed with the regulative procedure of reflective judgment" (p. 261fn.). And in his discussion of the three leaves in question, Friedman had stated that "in loose-leaf 3/4 Kant begins to characterize the *Transition* project in a strikingly new way: namely, as a doctrine of *natural investiga-*

tion [*Naturforschung*]" (p. 248). But this will hardly help to explain Kant's sudden realization of a gap. Apart from the fact that Kant speaks of *Naturforschung* already in the first draft of the *Opus postumum,* the *Oktaventwurf* of 1796 (21:404, Op. 17), the term is of course also employed in the Appendix to the Transcendental Dialectic to describe the role of the regulative ideas of reason (e.g., A694, 697, 699). Once again we are forced to the conclusion that, if this were the correct explanation of the gap in Kant's system, it must have existed already in 1781, in the *Critique of Pure Reason* itself. (For Kant's use of the term *Naturforschung* prior to 1798, see also A798, 816, 826; 5:360, 412, 428fn, 441; 8:159, 160, 163, 169, 180; 11:142.)

FOUR Ether Proof and *Selbstsetzungslehre*

1. Erich Adickes, *Kants Opus postumum dargestellt und beurteilt* (Berlin: Reuther & Reichard, 1920), p. 668.
2. Ibid., p. 699.
3. Similarly H. J. de Vleeschauwer, who writes with regard to self-positing: "Kant has bowed before the spirit of the time ... The infinite contortions of the *Opus postumum* serve to hide a conviction and basically to conceal a defeat" *(The Development of Kantian Thought* [London: Thomas Nelson and Sons, 1962], p. 189).
4. For a discussion of these *Reflexionen,* see Paul Guyer, *Kant and the Claims of Knowledge* (New York: Cambridge University Press, 1987), pt. 4.
5. On this point, see esp. Dieter Henrich, *Der ontologische Gottesbeweis* (Tübingen: J. C. B. Mohr, 1960); Tillman Pinder, "Kants Gedanke vom Grund aller Möglichkeiten" (Ph.D. diss., Freie Universität Berlin, 1969); Josef Schmucker, *Kants vorkritische Kritik der Gottesbeweise* (Wiesbaden: Franz Steiner, 1983).
6. "*Determinare* est ponere praedicatum cum exclusione oppositi" (1:391; cf. A598).
7. Paul Guyer, in his "Kant's Ether Deductions and the Possibility of Experience," in Gerhard Funke, ed., *Akten des Siebten Internationalen Kant-Kongresses* (Bonn: Bouvier, 1991), pp. 119–132, distinguishes "at least four different ar-

guments" for the existence of an ether in Kant (pp. 121f.). I prefer to speak of different strands within Kant's argument because I think that there is fundamentally only one proof for the ether, although Kant tried out a number of different presentations, as he did also with the deduction of the categories. In the present context, at any rate, my concern is with the overall structure of Kant's proof.

8. I am indebted to Johannes Haag for several helpful discussions of Kant's ether proof.

9. Thus Kant does not assert here that there can be no empty space, but says only that it could not be an object of possible experience: "An empty space is thinkable but not sensible" (21:235.28). For an argument why within Kant's dynamical theory of matter empty spaces are impossible on physical grounds, see Martin Carrier, "Kraft und Wirklichkeit," in Forum für Philosophie Bad Homburg, ed., *Übergang: Untersuchungen zum Spätwerk Immanuel Kants* (Frankfurt: Vittorio Klostermann, 1991), p. 210.

10. "For, were there a gap between them [i.e., perceptions], a gulf *(hiatus)* would [prevent] the transition from one act of existence to another, and the unity of the guiding thread of experience would be torn apart. Which circumstance, in order to be represented to oneself, would, in turn, have to belong to experience—which is impossible, for nonbeing can be no object of experience" (22:552, Op. 88).

11. "The concept of this material is the *basis* for the a priori connection of all the moving forces of matter, without which no unity in the relation of this manifold of forces in a single whole of matter could be thought" (21:229, Op. 76).

12. "In virtue of this all-penetration, the unity of this material (as of space itself) is the highest principle for the possibility of experience of outer sensible beings" (21:228, Op. 75).

13. "The proposition: 'There are physical bodies' presupposes the proposition: 'There is matter whose moving forces and motion precedes the generation of a body in time.' For this latter is only the formation of matter, and occurs of its own accord *(spontaneo)*. This formation, however, which is to be initiated by matter itself, must have a first beginning—whose possibility is, indeed, incomprehensible, but whose

originality (as self-activity) is not to be doubted" (21:216, Op. 68).

14. "Caloric is the matter distributed in space that cannot be thought to exist as an aggregate of parts, but only in [the form of] a system" (21:553.18–20).

15. It is the only candidate because the ether or caloric is "the hypostatized space itself, as it were" (21:224, Op. 73), of which there can only be one. Caloric is "thought of in such a way that, if one takes away everything that is movable in space, it nevertheless remains in the same place" (21:533.26f.).

16. In other sketches of the ether proof, Kant offers different conclusions for this second step. For example: "What belongs to the unity of *possible* experience, formally, is also contained really in experience; that is, the whole of this material is actual and an object of physics" (21:583, Op. 91). Or: "There is to be found here a *collective unity (omnitudo collectiva)* of the objects of a *single* experience instead of the *distributive* unity *(omnitudo distributiva)* . . . Whatever agrees with collective unity is *actual (existentia est omnimoda determinatio,* as ontology has it)" (21:586, Op. 93). I favor the conclusion given in my reconstruction of Kant's proof because it seems to me to offer the best chances for an integration of the ether proof into the general framework of the critical philosophy.

17. I thus disagree with Burkhard Tuschling's assessment of the ether in his *Metaphysische und transzendentale Dynamik in Kants opus postumum* (Berlin: de Gruyter, 1971), p. 175: "But what is this ether? . . . Is this concept of a non-empirical object a concept that is even possible within the classical critical theory of a priori knowledge? The answer is a clear 'No.'" See also Tuschling's "Apperception and Ether: On the Idea of a Transcendental Deduction of Matter in Kant's *Opus postumum*," in Eckart Förster, ed., *Kant's Transcendental Deductions: The Three 'Critiques' and the 'Opus postumum'* (Stanford: Stanford University Press, 1989), pp. 207, 213.

18. Compare also 21:597.4–15: "One cannot [procede] from an aggregate of perceptions (as moving forces of matter) to a system of them in one experience; rather, one must commence with the idea of a system of moving forces in the unity of experience, as the basis of the whole of the moving

forces, in order to represent to oneself the whole of one single experience not merely as thought but as given. However, what is represented as given in experience—and what must necessarily be thought so—must be thought of as existing. Hence there exists such a material as the basis of the moving forces of matter, and its existence is recognized in accordance with the principle of identity, as analytically contained in the unity of possible experience, not as depending synthetically on experience."

19. See Adickes, *Kants Opus postumum*, p. 139.

20. See J. H. Tieftrunk, "Anhang zur Prüfung des Beweisgrundes," in *Imanuel [sic] Kants vermischte Schriften* (Halle, 1797), 2:230–246.

21. See J. A. H. Ulrich, *Institutiones Logicae et Metaphysicae* (Jena, 1785), §§349, 351, pt. 2, §51; Moses Mendelssohn, *Morgenstunden, oder Vorlesungen über das Daseyn Gottes* (Berlin, 1785), Lecture 17, pp. 308–330.

22. In the Preface to his edition, Tieftrunk writes: "I noticed that several readers of the *Critique of Pure Reason* have found missing in it the examination and assessment of the 'One Possible Basis for a Demonstration of God's Existence,' and have hence declared the *Critique* incomplete. Therefore, in an Appendix to the said essay, I have tried to show that the missing 'Basis' is properly none other than the ontological [proof]—not, however, as it is usually given but as it ought to be given" (p. xi). The Preface is dated January 10, 1799.

23. See Kant's *Reflexionen* 3717, 3888, 4033 (17:260, 328, 391). See also Henrich, *Der ontologische Gottesbeweis*, pp. 185–188.

24. See, for example, 21:226, Op. 74. It is thus at best misleading to say, as Mathieu does, that Kant's ether proof is a new ontological proof. See Vittorio Mathieu, "Äther und Organismus in Kants 'Opus postumum,'" in H. Heimsoeth, D. Henrich, and G. Tonelli, eds., *Studien zu Kants philosophischer Entwicklung* (Heidelberg: Georg Olms, 1967), p. 186.

25. Vittorio Mathieu, *Kants Opus postumum* (Frankfurt: Klostermann, 1989), pp. 59–61, questions that Kant had the copy made "for the printer," and he does so for two reasons. First, in his manuscript Kant changed the expression "in sofern das Subject durch sie (sc. die Kräfte) vereinigt afficirt wird äußerlich und innerlich" to "in sofern das Subject durch sie äußerlich und innerlich in Einen Begriff vereinigt

sich selbst afficirt" (21:572.23). The altered version is then used in the amanuensis's copy. Of this Mathieu writes: "Since the doctrine of self-affection was only developed in 1799, the . . . alteration shows that Kant had the copy made later, *after* his position had changed. It is unlikely that Kant intended publication of the copy." Also, in the copied text Kant left the word "Second" (division) unchanged (22:549, Op. 86), apparently without noticing that the first division (see 21:565.17) had meanwhile been omitted—"an oversight," Mathieu writes, "that is inconceivable in a printer's copy [*Druckvorlage*], even with an author as absentminded as Kant" (p. 59). But is this really so inconceivable? After all, even in the printer's copy for the *Critique of Judgment* Kant had overlooked that the Deduction of Pure Aesthetic Judgment cannot be the "Dritter Abschnitt" (Division III) of the Analytic of Aesthetic Judgment—an "oversight" that later annoyed him considerably (see 11:139, 154). Mathieu's other example also is questionable. For Kant developed a theory of self-affection as early as the second edition of the first *Critique* (see B68–69 and 152–156). That the alteration at 21:572.23 (and hence the copy) *can only* have been made *after* fascicles 10 and 11 thus seems doubtful.

26. On the "Loses Blatt Leipzig 1" that Werner Stark discovered in 1989 and that belongs to the same phase of the *Opus postumum,* Kant had written in a similar vein: "The moving forces of matter that can be known a priori are those principles of its motion according to which we ourselves make the motion synthetically, as causes, not think it analytically; for the other [principles] yield only empirical laws of motion and belong to physics, not to the transition from metaphysics and the tendency of metaphysics to physics." See Werner Stark, "Loses Blatt Leipzig 1: Transkription und Bemerkungen," in *Übergang. Untersuchungen zum Spätwerk Immanuel Kants,* Herausgegeben vom Forum für Philosphie Bad Homburg (Frankfurt am Main: Klostermann, 1991), p. 146.

27. Two qualifications are perhaps in order. First, although the term *Selbstsetzungslehre* has become widely used for this part of the *Opus postumum,* what Kant presents the reader with is not a fully developed *Lehre,* or doctrine, but a systematic sketch of how the subject originally constitutes itself

as an object of experience. It is thus also not to be mistaken for a "phenomenology of embodiment" in the sense of Maurice Merleau-Ponty, Martin Heidegger, Hermann Schmitz, and others. Second, what Kant says at *Prolegomena* §21a with regard to the transcendental inquiry in general is of course also true of the *Selbstsetzungslehre,* namely, "that we are discussing not the origin of experience but what lies in experience" (4:304). The different steps in the argument described in the text thus are meant to indicate conceptually distinct levels, not temporally successive steps.

28. "Motion, considered as the description of a space, is a pure act of the successive synthesis of the manifold of outer intuition in general by means of the productive imagination, and belongs not only to geometry, but even to transcendental philosophy" (B155fn.).

29. The pulley is in fact not itself a simple machine but a circular derivative of the lever.

30. F. W. J. Schelling, *Ideas for a Philosophy of Nature,* trans. Errol E. Harris and Peter Heath (Cambridge: Cambridge University Press, 1988), p. 36.

31. See B129: a sensible intuition is "nothing but receptivity."

32. "The affectability of the subject as appearance is combined with the incitability of the corresponding moving forces, as correlate in perception" (22:396.15–17).

33. "In regard to matter and those of its forces which affect the subject (hence, are moving forces), perceptions are themselves moving forces combined with reaction *(reactio),* and the understanding *anticipates* perception according to the uniquely possible forms of motion" (22:502, Op. 146).

FIVE The Subject as Person and the Idea of God

1. On this point, see the fine discussion in Henry E. Allison, *Kant's Theory of Freedom* (Cambridge: Cambridge University Press, 1990), pp. 148f.

2. For the moral law prescribes that we take as one of our duties the happiness of others and further "what is best in the world, alike in ourselves and in others" (A819).

3. Compare Kant's *Lectures on Ethics* (trans. Louis Infield [New York: Harper & Row, 1963]), p. 55: "If only all men

united to promote one another's happiness we could make a paradise of Nowaya Zemlya [that is, an island in the Arctic Ocean; cf. 9:435]. God has set us on the stage where we can make one another happy. It depends on us, and us alone, to do so."

4. All quotations are from Garve's original review, reprinted in Kant's *Prolegomena,* ed. Rudolf Malter (Stuttgart: Reclam, 1989), pp. 237–238, 240.

5. Johann Georg Hamann, *Briefwechsel,* ed. Arthur Henkel (Frankfurt: Insel, 1965), 5:107.

6. Ibid., p. 129.

7. Ibid., p. 134.

8. Ibid., p. 141.

9. Ibid., p. 147.

10. Ibid., p. 402.

11. To my knowledge, Klaus Reich was the first to notice this, although he comes to conclusions that are quite different from mine. See his *Kant und die Ethik der Griechen* (Tübingen: J. C. B. Mohr [Paul Siebeck], 1935), pp. 27–48; English trans. by W. H. Walsh, "Kant and Greek Ethics (II)," *Mind* (1939), 446–463. A. R. C. Duncan, *Practical Reason and Morality* (London: Thomas Nelson and Sons, 1957), chap. 11, suggests that the different formulations of the categorical imperative in Part 2 of the *Groundwork* reflect Garve's impact on Kant. This thought is taken up by Brendan E. A. Liddell, who sees in these different formulations "Kant's attempt to incorporate the principles of Cicero (*per* Garve's notes) into his a priori moral system" (*Kant on the Foundation of Morality: A Modern Version of the Grundlegung* [Bloomington: Indiana University Press, 1970], p. 139). See also Pierre Laberge, "Du passage de la philosophie morale populaire à la métaphysique des moeurs," *Kant-Studien* 71 (1980), 418–444.

12. See also Paul Müller, "Chr. Garves Moralphilosophie und seine Stellungnahme zu Kants Ethik" (Ph.D. diss., Erlangen University, 1905).

13. Instead Feder writes: "We had better skip *how* the author proposes to found common thinking on moral concepts after he has deprived it of its speculative [concepts], because this we understand least of all." (Quoted in *Prolegomena,* Malter ed., p. 198.)

14. See Kant's "Vorarbeiten zu den *Prolegomena*," ibid., p. 187, and Kant's letter to Moses Mendelssohn of August 16, 1783—five days before he received Garve's original review: "This coming winter I will complete the first part of my morals, if not in its entirety, then at least the larger part of it" (10:346).

15. Neither did any of the forty-one words with the *Pflicht*-stem listed in the *Wortindex zu Kants gesammelten Schriften* (Berlin: de Gruyter, 1967), 2:697f. The word *Pflicht* occurs only four times in the first *Critique,* and always in a non-moral sense (A263, 589, 703, 726).

16. Christian Garve, *Philosophische Anmerkungen und Abhandlungen zu Cicero's Büchern von den Pflichten,* in *Garves Gesammelte Werke* (Neudruck Hildesheim: Georg Olms Verlag, 1986), 10:10.

17. See Moses Mendelssohn, *Morgenstunden oder Vorlesungen über das Dasein Gottes* (Berlin: Christian Friedrich Voss und Sohn, 1785), pp. 164f., and *An die Freunde Lessings* (Berlin: Christian Friedrich Voss und Sohn, 1786), pp. 33 and 67.

18. Interestingly, in the first *Critique* Kant does not recognize any dialectic of practical reason and thus can assign a *canon* to it (A796f.). In the *Groundwork,* by contrast, and taught better by the example of Garve's review of the *Critique,* Kant admits a natural dialectic "to quibble with that strict law of duty" (4:405). In the *Critique of Practical Reason,* because of the revised concept of happiness, practical reason even has to fend off a proper antinomy.

19. See also Pauline Kleingeld, *Fortschritt und Vernunft: Zur Geschichtsphilosophie Kants* (Würzburg: Königshausen & Neumann, 1995), p. 147.

20. The reason why, according to Kant, an ethical commonwealth cannot be realized by mankind alone is the "peculiar weakness of human nature" that it cannot convince itself "that steadfast zeal in the conduct of a morally good life is all that God requires of them to be his well-pleasing subjects in his Kingdom. They cannot indeed conceive their obligation except as directed to some *service* or other which they must perform for God" (6:103). Because of this propensity to a religion of divine worship, it so happens "that human beings will never regard either union into a church, or agree-

ment over the form to be given to it . . . as themselves necessary for the promotion of the moral element in religion"
(6:106). This remark also suggests, it seems to me, that the
realization of the ethical commonwealth through God
would have to amount to an externally induced change of
human dispositions. Yet in the Preface to the *Religion* Kant
already writes: "All men *could have* sufficient incentive [in
the moral law] if *(as they ought to)* they adhered solely to
the dictates of pure reason in the law" (6:7fn.; my italics).
For "ought" implies "can." Instead, men seek a "consequence" *(Erfolg)* for their actions that they can "love." See
also 6:108: "The common man" always needs "his ecclesias-
tical faith, which appeals to his senses, whereas religion is
hidden within and depends on moral dispositions."

21. See also J. Bohatec, *Die Religionsphilosophie Kants in der "Religion innerhalb der Grenzen der bloßen Vernunft"* (1938;
reprint, Hildesheim: Georg Olms, 1966), pp. 484–487.

22. "We cannot very well make obligation (moral necessitation)
tangible to ourselves without thereby thinking of *another*
person, namely God, and of His will (of which universally
legislative reason is only the spokesman)" (6:487).

23. As it was in classical antiquity; see Klaus Düsing, "Das
Problem des höchsten Gutes in Kants praktischer Philosophie," *Kant-Studien* 62 (1971), 5–54.

24. Ibid.

SIX "I Regard Reason as the Beginning
     of the Understanding"

1. F. H. Jacobi, "Über die Lehre des Spinoza, in Briefen an
   Herrn Moses Mendelssohn," in F. Roth and F. Köppen, eds.,
   Jacobis Werke, (Darmstadt: Wissenschaftliche Buchgesell-
   schaft, 1968), 4:xxi, xxxviii.

2. See Dieter Henrich, *Der Grund im Bewußtsein: Untersuchungen zu Hölderlins Denken (1794–1795)* (Stuttgart:
   Klett-Cotta, 1992), esp. pt. 1.

3. See J. G. Hamann, "Aesthetica in nuce," in *Sämtliche Werke,*
   ed. Josef Nadler (Vienna: Herder, 1950), 2:197. That Hölderlin is the author of the "Oldest System Program" I argued in
   "'To Lend Wings to Physics once Again': Hölderlin and the

'Oldest System Programme of German Idealism,'" *European Journal of Philosophy* (1995), 174–198.

4. See also Dieter Henrich, "Hölderlin on Judgment and Being," in Eckart Förster, ed., *The Course of Remembrance and Other Essays on Hölderlin* (Stanford: Stanford University Press, 1997), pp. 71–89.

5. It would also be misguided to see such a reversal take place in the Appendix to the Transcendental Dialectic. For there, too, it is the case that "reason presupposes the knowledge which is obtained by the understanding" (A662). And when Kant declares that without similarity among the appearances that present themselves to us no concept formation was possible, "and the understanding itself, which has to do solely with such concepts, would be non-existent" (A654), what is presupposed thereby is similarity among the representations of sense, not the idea of reason of such similarity. This idea, together with its associated ideas of variety and affinity, comes after the understanding has gained its cognitions.

6. "Kant was the first to emphasize the distinction between understanding and reason in a definite way, establishing the finite and conditioned as the subject matter of the former, and the infinite and unconditioned as that of the latter." G. W. F. Hegel, *Enzyclopedie*, §45 Addition, trans. T. F. Geraets, W. A. Suchting, and H. S. Harris (Indianapolis: Hackett Publishing Company, 1991), p. 88.

7. See Wolfgang Welsch, *Vernunft* (Frankfurt: Suhrkamp, 1995), pp. 804–820.

8. See also Manfred Baum, "Kants kritischer Rationalismus: Zur Entwicklung des Vernunftbegriffs nach 1770," in H. F. Fulda and R.-P. Horstmann, eds., *Vernunftbegriffe in der Moderne* (Stuttgart: Klett-Cotta, 1994), pp. 184–198.

9. See J. W. von Goethe, *Faust: A Tragedy*, pt. 1 (1808), "Study," l. 1237.

10. See also Ulrich Steinvorth, "Wittgensteins transzendentale Definition der ostensiven Definition," *Kant-Studien* 60 (1969), 494–505.

11. See W. V. O. Quine, "Ontological Relativity," in *Ontological Relativity and Other Essays* (New York: Columbia University Press, 1969), p. 31.

12. *Philosophical Review* 77 (1968), 275–320, 314; also in Ludwig Wittgenstein, *Philosophical Occasions, 1912–1951* (Indianapolis: Hackett, 1993).

13. The problem of the inner-outer distinction occupied Wittgenstein almost to the end of his life. See Ludwig Wittgenstein, *Last Writings on the Philosophy of Psychology*, vol. 2, ed. G. H. von Wright and Heikki Nyman (Oxford: Blackwell, 1992).

14. Compare the remarks concerning the unavoidable ambiguity of the expression "outside me" in the *Critique of Pure Reason*, A373.

Index

categorical imperative, 117,
139–140, 144, 145, 170, 196n11;
as figment of the brain, 125; as
principle of unification, 131,
137, 138, 140–141, 144; as voice
of God, 143

categories, 4, 13–15, 56–58, 61,
66, 67, 83, 89, 111, 113, 114,
125, 149, 150, 156, 158; objective reality of, 57–59, 61–62,
72–74

chemistry, 2, 71–72; revolution
of, 2

Cicero, Marcus Tullius, 123–126,
196n11

circle, in theory of matter, 2,
34–37, 42, 43, 45, 66, 71, 115,
181–183n13

cohesion, 3, 16, 18, 20, 43–46,
66–68, 70–71, 83, 110, 111, 115;
law of, 66–67, 71

construction, 36–37, 39–41,
61–63, 65, 66, 69–72, 74, 113,
114, 115, 182n13, 187n21

critical philosophy, 48, 51, 53, 56,
57, 60, 69, 72–73, 75, 79, 115,
189n24

Darwin, Erasmus, 105

density, 15, 72; differences of,
33–35, 41, 43, 46, 66, 68, 71

Descartes, René, 32

Düsing, Klaus, 198nn23,24

Duncan, A. R. C., 196n11

Duque, Felix, 25

duty, 116, 126, 129, 131, 132, 133,
136, 137, 139, 140, 141, 153,
158, 159, 161, 162, 163, 179n15;
as divine command, 117,
136, 142, 143; laws of, 145;

imperative of, 161; as moving
force in the world, 161

elementary system of forces, 11,
18, 20, 21, 83, 98, 99–100, 112,
113, 114, 116, 157; principle of
99; topoi of, 116

ether, 14, 29, 32, 42–47, 67, 68, 77,
83, 85, 110, 113, 116, 141, 162,
163, 172; as pulsating, 45–47,
67, 71, 97; as stratified, 46–47;
as hypothesis, 83, 93; as hypostatized space, 87, 99, 105, 110;
as ideal, 91–93, 96, 99, 111, 116;
attributes of, 93, 96–99,
110–112, 116. See also caloric

ether proof, 82, 86–93, 95, 96, 99,
100, 105–106, 110, 157, 158,
193n24; subjective step of,
88–90, 99, 100; objective step
of, 88–91, 99

Euclid, 104

Euler, Leonhard, 29–32, 46–47,
181n10

excitability. See sensibility

experience, 60, 70, 98, 124, 144;
possibility of, 16, 83, 86, 87–90,
93, 96–99, 105, 110–111, 116,
157, 191n12; principle of, 17;
as all-embracing, 81, 86, 87, 92,
113, 116; collective unity of, 81,
82, 88, 89, 99, 172, 192n16; system of, 84, 88; whole of, 86, 87,
88, 90, 91, 93, 177n5; distributive unity of, 88, 192n16; definition of, 89; unity of, 97, 101

Fambach, Oscar, 183n17

Faust, Heinrich, 158

Feder, Johann Georg Heinrich,
122, 196n13
Fichte, Johann Gottlieb, 75, 76
Fischer, Kuno, 49, 184n3
Flittner, Christian Gottfried,
185n7
forces, 66, 105–107, 111–112, 161,
162; system of, 11, 17, 21,
66–67, 84, 192n18; specific variety of, 12, 100; living, 13,
43–45, 67; moving, 13, 17, 18,
20, 21, 27, 67, 70, 83, 93, 101,
112, 138, 159, 170; dynamical,
16, 83, 110; mechanical, 20–21,
83, 108, 110; organic, 21, 22, 25,
26, 28, 74, 106; fundamental,
number of, 34, 37–41, 62–63,
184n13; collective unity of,
83–86, 88–89, 106; distributive
unity of, 83, 85, 86; basis of, 86,
87, 88, 96, 105, 158, 191n11;
topic of, 99, 100, 111, 157;
knowability of, 100, 157,
194n26
freedom, 55, 118, 128, 138, 139,
141, 144, 160, 162, 170; of understanding, 9; law of, 139, 141;
practical, 139
free play of faculties, 9–10
Friedman, Michael, 1, 2–3, 7–8,
11, 178nn7,12,13, 179n14,
182n13, 185n6, 186n15,
187nn19,21, 188n24
Fulda, Hans Friedrich, 199n8
Funke, Gerhard, 190n7

Galilei, Galileo, 67, 187n22
Garve, Christian, 48–50, 52–53,
68, 69, 73, 122–126,
196nn4,11,12, 197nn14,16,18

Gehler, Johann Samuel Traugott,
16, 22–23, 38, 179n21, 180n24
Genz, Friedrich, 26
Geraets, Théodore F., 199n6
Gloy, Karen, 177n1
god, 55, 79, 82, 119, 121, 123, 125,
133, 136, 138, 141, 145, 146,
150, 162, 163, 170, 172; existence of, 77–78, 94–96, 135,
137, 141, 142, 146; as ideal, 82,
141, 143, 144; attributes of, 96,
130; as omnipotent, 118, 137; as
author, 120, 122, 125, 130; as
moral ruler, 120, 128, 130, 132,
134, 137, 140–142, 144, 172; as
incentive, 120, 124, 125; as postulate, 121, 129, 130, 132,
134–135, 147, 173, 174; moral
people of, 131, 135, 137, 140; as
moral lawgiver, 134, 136, 137;
as inner vital spirit of man, 173,
174
Goethe, Johann Wolfgang von,
199n9
Gok, Karl (Hölderlin's brother),
153
Guyer, Paul, 178n12, 190nn4,7

Haag, Johannes, 191n8
Haller, Albrecht von, 105
Hamann, Johann Georg, 123,
151, 196nn5–10, 198n3
happiness, 118–122, 124, 126, 131,
132, 140; moral, 119, 121, 129,
135; empirical, 119, 120, 129,
135; in proportion to virtue,
120, 128, 130, 131, 134, 135
Harris, Errol E., 183n21, 195n30
Harris, Henry Silton, 199n6
heat, 15, 47, 110